VEGAN MEALS

10 9 8 7 6 5 4 3 2 1

BBC Books, an imprint of Ebury Publishing
20 Vauxhall Bridge Road,
London SW1V 2SA

BBC Books is part of the Penguin Random House
group of companies whose addresses can be
found at global.penguinrandomhouse.com

Photographs © BBC Magazines 2019
Recipes © BBC Worldwide 2019
Book design © Woodlands Books Ltd 2019
All recipes contained in this book first appeared
in BBC *Good Food* magazine.

First published by BBC Books in 2019

www.eburypublishing.co.uk

A CIP catalogue record for this book is avail-
able from the British Library

ISBN 978 1 785 94397 3

Colour origination by BORN Ltd
Typeset in 10/12 pt Century Gothic
by Integra Software Services Pvt. Ltd
Printed and bound in China by C&C Offset
Printing Co, Ltd.

Cover Design: Interstate Creative Partners Ltd
Production: Rebecca Jones

BBC Books would like to thank the following
people for providing photos. While every effort
has been made to trace and acknowledge
all photographers, we should like to apologise
should there be any errors or omissions.

Image credits:
Emma Boyns 203, 233; Peter Cassidy 197, 205,
219; Mike English 25, 27, 29, 43, 45, 47, 51, 53, 69,
75, 81, 89, 93, 97, 105, 107, 109, 113, 119, 123,
137, 139, 167, 225; Sam Folan 73; Will Heap 9, 11,
13, 15, 19, 33, 79, 87, 111, 115, 125, 129, 145, 153,
155, 157, 179, 199, 213, 215, 221, 223, 227, 229,
231, 235, 237; Lara Holmes 161; Adrian Law-
rence 59; Gareth Morgans 151; David Munns 83,
149, 211; Myles New 193; Stuart Ovenden 65, 71,
121, 131, 147, 195; Lis Parsons 21; Tom Regester
49, 55, 61, 63, 67, 77, 91, 117, 135, 141, 143,
163, 165, 169, 171, 173, 177, 181, 183, 187, 201,
207, 217; Toby Scott 159; Maja Smend 57;
Sam Stowell 101; Rob Streeter 17, 31, 35, 37, 39,
99, 103, 127, 189, 191; Clare Winfield 95, 185.

All the recipes in this book were created by the
editorial team at *Good Food* and by regular
contributors to BBC Magazines.

Contents

Introduction, notes & conversions

INTRODUCTION

Vegan diets are becoming more and more popular, with many vegetarians and meat eaters ditching animal products in favour of veg and grain-packed diets. Going vegan has become much easier in the past few years, with the introduction of a variety of dairy and meat substitutions hitting the supermarket shelves. Coconut, soya and nut milks, yoghurts, butters and oils are easy to get hold of. Other more unusual ingredients, such as seitan and nutritional yeast, can be found in health food shops or online.

One thing you never have to worry about when cooking a *Good Food* recipe is if the recipe will work. We triple test all of our recipes in our development kitchen, tweaking and adapting until it's just right, meaning all you have to do is follow the recipe for perfect results. The recipes in this book are all nutritionally analysed by a qualified nutritionist.

Whether you're a full-time vegan, or simply want to start introducing more plant-based meals into your diet, this book has something for everyone. The recipes are easy to follow and offer solutions for everything from everyday dinners the whole family will love to sweet treats (that no one will guess are vegan). Enjoy a new, healthier style of cooking and pack in more of the good stuff with this book full of inspiring recipes. Happy cooking!

NOTES ON THE RECIPES
- Wash fresh produce before preparation.
- Recipes contain nutritional analyses for 'sugars', which means the total sugar content including all natural sugars in the ingredients, unless otherwise stated.

APPROXIMATE LIQUID CONVERSION

Metric	Imperial	Aus	US
50ml	2 fl oz	¼ cup	¼ cup
125ml	4 fl oz	½ cup	½ cup
175ml	6 fl oz	¾ cup	¾ cup
225ml	8 fl oz	1 cup	1 cup
300ml	10 fl oz/½ pint	½ pint	1¼ cups
450ml	16 fl oz	2 cups	2 cups/1 pint
600ml	20 fl oz/1 pint	1 pint	2½ cups
1 litre	35 fl oz/1¾ pints	1¾ pints	1 quart

OVEN TEMPERATURE CONVERSION

GAS	°C	°C FAN	°F	OVEN TEMP.
¼	110	90	225	Very cool
½	120	100	250	Very cool
1	140	120	275	Cool or slow
2	150	130	300	Cool or slow
3	160	140	325	Warm
4	180	160	350	Moderate
5	190	170	375	Moderately hot
6	200	180	400	Fairly hot
7	220	200	425	Hot
8	230	210	450	Very hot
9	240	220	475	Very hot

APPROXIMATE WEIGHT CONVERSIONS

Cup measurements, which are used in Australia and America, have not been listed here as they vary from ingredient to ingredient. Kitchen scales should be used to measure dry/solid ingredients.

SPOON MEASURES

Spoon measurements are level unless otherwise specifed.
- 1 teaspoon (tsp) = 5ml
- 1 tablespoon (tbsp) = 15ml
- 1 Australian tablespoon = 20ml (cooks in Australia should measure 3 teaspoons where 1 tablespoon is specifed in a recipe)

CHAPTER 1: BREAKFAST & BRUNCH

Start the day the right way with a healthy dose of fruits and vegetables. Whether you fancy something quick and easy, or a special brunch for the weekend, you'll find plenty of inspiration in this chapter. A smoothie bowl is a great way to start the day – it's a thicker version of a smoothie, served in a bowl and topped with fresh fruit, seeds and nuts; it looks and tastes great. Or for something more indulgent, try our vegan fry-up.

Chive waffles with maple & soy mushrooms

These delicious vegan waffles can be sweet or savoury and are super adaptable to every taste. A great low-calorie breakfast or brunch option.

 TAKES 45 mins ⏲ SERVES 6

- 500ml soya milk or rice milk
- 1 tsp cider vinegar or lemon juice
- 2 tbsp rapeseed oil
- 100g cooked, mashed sweet potato
- 150g polenta
- 130g plain flour
- 1 tbsp baking powder
- small bunch chives, snipped
- 1 tbsp maple syrup
- 2 tsp light soy sauce
- 6 large mushrooms, thickly sliced
- olive oil, for frying
- soya yoghurt, to serve (optional)

1 Heat the waffle iron. Mix the soya or rice milk with the vinegar and rapeseed oil (don't worry if it starts to split), then whisk in the sweet potato mash. Tip the polenta, flour and baking powder into a bowl, mix and make a well in the centre. Add a large pinch of salt, then slowly pour in the milk mixture and whisk to make a batter. Stir in half of the chives.

2 Pour enough batter into the waffle iron to fill and cook for 4–5 mins. Lift out the waffle, keep it warm and repeat with the remaining mixture until you have 6 waffles.

3 Meanwhile, mix the maple syrup with the soy sauce. Brush it over the mushrooms and season with pepper. Heat a little oil in a frying pan and fry the mushrooms on both sides until they are browned and cooked through – make sure they don't burn at the edges. Serve the waffles topped with mushrooms, add a spoonful of soya yoghurt, if you like, and scatter over the remaining chives.

Nutrition per serving
Kcals 227 • fat 8g • saturates 1g • carbs 30g • sugars 7g • fibre 4g • protein 7g • salt 1.2g

Vegan fry-up

Try this vegan take on the classic English breakfast that boasts vegan sausages with hash browns, mushrooms, tomatoes, scrambled tofu and baked beans.

 TAKES 45 mins SERVES 2

FOR THE HASH BROWNS
- 1 large potato, unpeeled
- 1½ tbsp peanut butter

FOR THE TOMATOES AND MUSHROOMS
- 14 cherry tomatoes
- sunflower oil
- 2 tsp maple syrup
- 1 tsp soy sauce
- ¼ tsp smoked paprika
- 1 large Portobello mushroom, sliced

FOR THE SCRAMBLED TOFU
- 349g pack silken tofu
- 2 tbsp nutritional yeast
- ½ tsp turmeric
- 1 garlic clove, crushed

TO SERVE
- 4 vegan sausages
- 200g can baked beans

1 Cook the potato whole in a large pan of water, boil for 10 mins then drain and allow to cool. Peel the skin away then coarsely grate. Mix with the peanut butter and season well. Set aside in the fridge until needed.

2 Heat oven to 200C/180C fan/gas 6. Put the cherry tomatoes onto a baking tray, drizzle with 2 tsp sunflower oil, season and bake for 30 mins, or until the skins have blistered and start to char. Cook the sausages and beans following the instructions on the pack so they're ready to serve at the same time as the scrambled tofu.

3 Meanwhile, mix the maple syrup, soy sauce and smoked paprika together in a large bowl, add the sliced mushroom and toss to coat in the mixture. Leave to stand while you pour 2 tsp sunflower oil into a non-stick frying pan and bring it up to a medium high heat. Fry the mushroom until just starting to turn golden but not charred. Scoop onto a plate and keep warm until ready to serve.

4 Put 1 tbsp oil into the frying pan and add spoonfuls of the potato mixture – you should get about 4. Fry for 3–4 mins each side then drain on kitchen paper.

5 Crumble the tofu into your frying pan and sprinkle over the remaining ingredients and a good pinch of salt and pepper. If the pan looks a little dry add a splash more oil. Fry for 3–4 mins, or until the tofu is broken into pieces, well coated in the seasoning and hot through.

6 Divide everything between 2 plates and serve with a hot mug of tea made using soya milk.

Nutrition per serving
Kcals 644 • fat 26g • saturates 4g • carbs 56g • sugars 19g • fibre 11g • protein 41g • salt 3.11g

Mexican beans & avocado on toast

A vibrant Mexican-style breakfast with fresh avocado and black beans. Give yourself a healthy start with our easy vegan beans on toast with a twist.

 TAKES 30 mins   SERVES 4

- 270g cherry tomatoes, quartered
- 1 red or white onion, finely chopped
- ½ lime, juiced
- 4 tbsp olive oil
- 2 garlic cloves, crushed
- 1 tsp ground cumin
- 2 tsp chipotle paste or 1 tsp chilli flakes
- 2 x 400g cans black beans, drained
- small bunch coriander, chopped
- 4 slices bread
- 1 avocado, finely sliced

1 Mix the tomatoes, ¼ onion, lime juice and 1 tbsp oil and set aside. Fry the remaining onion in 2 tbsp oil until it starts to soften. Add the garlic, fry for 1 min, then add the cumin and chipotle and stir until fragrant. Tip in the beans and a splash of water, stir and cook gently until heated through. Stir in most of the tomato mixture and cook for 1 min, season well and add most of the coriander.
2 Toast the bread and drizzle with the remaining 1 tbsp oil. Put a slice on each plate and pile some beans on top. Arrange some slices of avocado on top, then sprinkle with the remaining tomato mixture and coriander leaves to serve.

Nutrition per serving
Kcals 368 • fat 19g • saturates 3g • carbs 30g • sugars 6g • fibre 13g • protein 12g • salt 0.9g

Breakfast muffins

Make muffins healthier with mashed banana and apple sauce for natural sweetness, plus blueberries and seeds for an extra nutritious hit.

TAKES 45 mins MAKES 12 muffins

- 1½ tbsp ground flaxseed
- 150ml pot dairy-free yoghurt
- 50ml rapeseed oil
- 100g apple sauce or puréed apples (find with the baby food)
- 1 ripe banana, mashed
- 4 tbsp maple syrup
- 1 tsp vanilla extract
- 200g wholemeal flour
- 50g rolled oats, plus extra for sprinkling
- 1½ tsp baking powder
- 1½ tsp bicarbonate of soda
- 1½ tsp cinnamon
- 100g blueberries
- 2 tbsp mixed seeds (we used pumpkin, sunflower and flaxseed)

1 Heat oven to 180C/160C fan/gas 4. Line a 12-hole muffin tin with 12 large muffin cases. In a jug, mix the flaxseed, yoghurt, oil, apple sauce, banana, maple syrup and vanilla. Tip the remaining ingredients, except the seeds, into a large bowl, add a pinch of salt and mix to combine.

2 Pour the wet ingredients into the dry and mix briefly until you have a smooth batter – don't overmix as this will make the muffins heavy. Divide the batter among the cases. Sprinkle the muffins with the extra oats and the seeds. Bake for 25–30 mins until golden and well risen, and a skewer inserted into the centre of a muffin comes out clean. Remove from the oven, transfer to a wire rack and leave to cool. Can be stored in a sealed container for up to 3 days.

Nutrition per serving
Kcals 179 • fat 7g • saturates 1g • carbs 23g • sugars 10g • fibre 3g • protein 5g • salt 0.6g

Cinnamon & blueberry French toast

This easy vegan version of French toast is best served golden brown and slathered with maple syrup and fresh fruit. The perfect indulgent brunch option.

 TAKES 40 mins SERVES 6

- 3 tbsp maple syrup
- 150g blueberries
- 2 tbsp gram flour
- 2 tbsp ground almonds
- 2 tsp cinnamon
- 200ml oat milk or rice milk
- 1 tbsp golden caster sugar
- 1 tsp vanilla extract
- grapeseed oil, for frying
- 6 slices thick white bread
- icing sugar, for dusting

1 Gently heat the maple syrup and blueberries in a saucepan until the berries start to pop and release their juices, then set them to one side in the pan. Whisk the flour, almonds, cinnamon, milk, sugar and vanilla together in a shallow bowl.

2 Heat a little oil in a frying pan. Dip a slice of bread into the milk mixture, shake off any excess and fry the bread on both sides until it browns and crisps at the edges. Keep the slices warm in a low oven as you cook the rest. Serve with the blueberries spooned over and dust with icing sugar.

Nutrition per serving
Kcals 210 • fat 6g • saturates 1g • carbs 32g • sugars 16g • fibre 2g • protein 5g • salt 0.3g

Coconut & banana pancakes

These coconut milk pancakes with passion fruit and banana topping couldn't be simpler.

🕐 TAKES 25 mins 🕑 SERVES 8–10

- 150g plain flour
- 2 tsp baking powder
- 3 tbsp golden caster sugar
- 400ml can coconut milk, shaken well
- vegetable oil, for frying
- 1–2 bananas, thinly sliced
- 2 passion fruits, flesh scooped out

1 Sift the flour and baking powder into a bowl and stir in 2 tbsp of the sugar and a pinch of salt. Pour the coconut milk into a bowl, whisk to mix in any fat that has separated, then measure out 300ml into a jug. Stir the milk slowly into the flour mixture to make a smooth batter, or whizz everything in a blender.

2 Heat a shallow frying pan or flat griddle and brush it with oil. Use 2 tbsp of batter to make each pancake, frying 2 at a time – any more will make it difficult to flip them. Push 4–5 pieces of banana into each pancake and cook until bubbles start to pop on the surface, and the edges look dry. They will be a little more delicate than egg-based pancakes, so turn them over carefully and cook the other sides for 1 min. Repeat to make 8–10 pancakes.

3 Meanwhile, put the remaining coconut milk and sugar in a small pan. Add a pinch of salt and simmer until the mixture thickens to the consistency of single cream. Use this as a sauce for the pancakes and serve with the remaining banana slices and the passion fruit seeds.

Nutrition per serving (10)
Kcals 179 • fat 8g • saturates 6g • carbs 23g • sugars 11g • fibre 1g • protein 2g • salt 0.2g

Vegan pancakes

Practise your flip to make our gluten-free pancakes. Buy hemp or coconut milk, egg replacer and gluten-free flour from supermarkets or health food shops.

⏱ TAKES 30 mins ◗ SERVES 6

- 125g gluten-free plain flour
- egg replacer, equivalent to 1 whole egg, mixed with 2 tbsp water
- 250ml hemp or coconut milk
- sunflower or rice bran oil, for frying
- lemon wedges and agave syrup or caster sugar, to serve

1 Put the flour in a bowl and make a well in the centre. Pour in the egg replacer and a quarter of the milk.
2 Use an electric whisk to thoroughly combine the mixture, then beat in another quarter of the milk. Once lump free, mix in the remaining milk. Leave to rest for 20 mins. Stir again before using.
3 Heat a small non-stick frying pan with a splash of oil. When hot pour a small amount of the mixture into the pan and swirl around to coat the base – you want a thin layer.
4 Cook for a few mins until golden brown on the bottom, then turn over and cook until golden on the other side. Repeat until you have used all the mixture, stirring the mixture between pancakes and adding more oil to the frying pan as necessary.
5 Serve with a lemon wedge and agave syrup or sugar or filling of your choice. This mixture keeps for a few days if you store it covered in the fridge. Give it a good whisk before using.

Nutrition per serving (using hemp milk)
Kcals 108 • fat 3g • saturates 0.3g • carbs 16.2g • sugars 0.7g • fibre 0.2g • protein 3.6g • salt 0g

Raspberry coconut porridge

This fruity porridge is dairy-free as it uses coconut yoghurt. Although healthy, the yoghurt is quite high in fat, so one pot is enough for four portions.

○ TAKES 20 mins plus overnight soaking ◖ SERVES 4

- 100g rolled porridge oats (not instant)
- 25g creamed coconut, chopped
- 200g frozen raspberries
- 125g pot coconut yoghurt
- a few mint leaves, to serve (optional)

1 Tip the oats and creamed coconut into a large bowl, pour on 800ml cold water, cover and leave to soak overnight.

2 The next day, tip the contents of the bowl into a saucepan and cook over a medium heat, stirring frequently, for 5–10 mins until the oats are cooked. Add the raspberries to the pan with the yoghurt and allow to thaw and melt into the oats off the heat. Spoon the porridge into bowls. Top each portion with mint leaves, if you like.

Nutrition per serving
Kcals 224 • fat 12g • saturates 9g • carbs 21g • sugars 3g • fibre 4g • protein 5g • salt 0g

Quinoa porridge

Supercharge your morning with high-protein quinoa and omega-3 rich chia seeds for a creamy breakfast bowl topped with seasonal fruit.

TAKES 35 mins plus overnight soaking • SERVES 4

FOR THE PORRIDGE (TO SERVE 4)
- 175g quinoa
- ½ vanilla pod, split and seeds scraped out, or ½ tsp vanilla extract
- 15g creamed coconut
- 4 tbsp chia seeds
- 125g coconut yoghurt

FOR THE TOPPING (TO SERVE 2)
- 125g coconut yoghurt
- 280g mixed summer berries, such as strawberries, raspberries and blueberries
- 2 tbsp flaked almonds (optional)

1 Activate the quinoa by soaking overnight in cold water. The next day, drain and rinse the quinoa through a fine sieve (the grains are so small that they will wash through a coarse one).

2 Tip the quinoa into a pan and add the vanilla, creamed coconut and 600ml water. Cover the pan and simmer for 20 mins. Stir in the chia with another 300ml water and cook gently for 3 mins more. Stir in the coconut yoghurt. Spoon half the porridge into a bowl for another day. Will keep for 2 days covered in the fridge. Serve the remaining porridge topped with another pot of yoghurt, the berries and almonds, if you like.

3 To have the porridge another day, tip into a pan and reheat gently, with vegan milk or water. Top with fruit – for instance, orange slices and pomegranate seeds.

Nutrition per serving
Kcals 446 • fat 24g • saturates 14g • carbs 40g • sugars 14g • fibre 9g • protein 12g • salt 0.1g

Maple baked granola

This is a good 'blueprint granola' – follow the basic premise then add nuts and dried fruits of your choosing. Will store in an airtight container for 2 weeks.

TAKES 50 mins MAKES about 1kg

- 300g four-grain porridge mix (containing oat, wheat, barley and rice flakes), or a multigrain porridge mix of your choice
- 50g crispy malted wheat flakes
- 50g crispy spelt flakes
- 50g each pecans, walnuts and unblanched hazelnuts, roughly chopped
- 150g mixed seeds (we used a pumpkin, sunflower and sesame mix)
- 15g hemp seeds (optional)
- 225ml maple syrup
- 4 tbsp hazelnut or walnut oil
- 100g dried apples, chopped
- 75g dried cranberries
- 75g dried sour cherries

1 Heat oven to 160C/140C fan/gas 3. Line 2 large roasting tins (or 1 and cook in batches) with baking parchment. Put the porridge mix and all the flakes, nuts and seeds in a bowl and mix them together.
2 Put the maple syrup and oil in a big heavy-bottomed saucepan and gently heat. Add the grain mixture and stir until all the dry ingredients are coated – you are not cooking the mixture, just coating it. Spread the cereal over the parchment (it shouldn't lie in big clumps) and bake for about 20 mins.
3 Remove the tins from the oven, turn the temperature up to 180C/160C fan/gas 4, then return to the oven, swapping the tins over. Cook for another 10 mins, but keep an eye on things. You want a golden toasted mixture – you may even start to smell some caramelisation – but don't take it too far.
4 Take the tins out of the oven and leave to cool. Break the granola up into small chunks with your hands and add the dried fruit. This will keep well in an airtight container for 2 weeks. You can 'refresh' it by putting it all in the oven again (at 160C/140C fan/gas 3) for 15 mins. Eat with vegan milk or yoghurt and fresh fruit.

Nutrition per serving
Kcals 121 • fat 6g • saturates 1g • carbs 12g • sugars 6g • fibre 2g • protein 3g • salt 0g

Chocolate chia pudding

Make a tasty, healthy chocolate pudding in just 5 minutes, perfect for a breakfast treat. It's low-calorie and the chia seeds are a great source of omega-3 fatty acids.

🕐 TAKES 5 mins plus overnight thickening 🥧 SERVES 4

- 60g chia seeds
- 400ml unsweetened almond milk or hazelnut milk
- 3 tbsp cacao powder
- 2 tbsp maple syrup
- ½ tsp vanilla extract
- frozen berries, to serve
- cacao nibs, to serve

1 Put all the ingredients in a large bowl with a generous pinch of sea salt and whisk to combine. Cover with cling film then leave to thicken in the fridge for at least 4 hours, or overnight.
2 Spoon the pudding into 4 glasses, then top with the frozen berries and cacao nibs.

Nutrition per serving
Kcals 130 • fat 7g • saturates 1g • carbs 9g • sugars 6g • fibre 7g • protein 4g • salt 0.3g

Summer porridge

A healthy, summery porridge with jumbo oats and bright pink pomegranate seeds.

🕐 TAKES 20 mins ⏾ SERVES 2

- 300ml almond milk
- 200g blueberries
- ½ tbsp maple syrup
- 2 tbsp chia seeds
- 100g jumbo oats
- 1 kiwi fruit, peeled and cut into slices
- 50g pomegranate seeds
- 2 tsp mixed seeds

1 In a blender, blitz the milk, blueberries and maple syrup until the milk turns purple. Put the chia and oats in a mixing bowl, pour in the blueberry milk and stir very well. Leave to soak for 5 mins, stirring occasionally, until the liquid has absorbed, and the oats and chia thicken and swell.

2 Stir again, then divide between 2 bowls. Arrange the fruit on top, then sprinkle over the mixed seeds. Will keep in the fridge for 1 day. Add the toppings just before serving.

Nutrition per serving
Kcals 391 • fat 12g • saturates 2g • carbs 49g • sugars 19g • fibre 14g • protein 14g • salt 0.2g

Kale smoothie

Give yourself a dose of vitamin C in the morning with this green smoothie. Along with kale and avocado, there's a hit of zesty lime and pineapple.

🕐 TAKES 5 mins 🕒 SERVES 2

- 2 handfuls kale
- ½ avocado
- ½ lime, juice only
- large handful frozen pineapple chunks
- medium-sized chunk ginger
- 1 tbsp cashew nuts
- 1 banana (optional)

1 Put all of the ingredients into a bullet or smoothie maker, add a large splash of water and blitz. Add more water until you have the desired consistency.

Nutrition per serving
Kcals 152 • fat 11g • saturates 2g • carbs 8g • sugars 3g • fibre 2g • protein 4g • salt 0.1g

Tropical smoothie bowl

Add a taste of the tropical to your breakfast with our easy vegan, mango and pineapple smoothie bowl.

 TAKES 20 mins SERVES 2

- 1 small ripe mango, stoned, peeled and cut into chunks
- 200g pineapple, peeled, cored and cut into chunks
- 2 ripe bananas
- 2 tbsp coconut yoghurt (not coconut-flavoured yoghurt)
- 150ml coconut drinking milk
- 2 passion fruits, halved, seeds scooped out
- handful blueberries
- 2 tbsp coconut flakes
- a few mint leaves

1 Put the mango, pineapple, bananas, yoghurt and coconut milk in a blender, and blitz until smooth and thick. Pour into 2 bowls and decorate with the passion fruit, blueberries, coconut flakes and mint leaves. Will keep in the fridge for 1 day. Add the toppings just before serving.

Nutrition per serving
Kcals 332 • fat 15g • saturates 13g • carbs 41g • sugars 38g • fibre 8g • protein 4g • salt 0.1g

Green Goddess smoothie bowl

Prepare this bowl of goodness the night before for a speedy breakfast bowl that's all 5 of your 5-a-day!

 TAKES 25 mins SERVES 2

- 1 ripe avocado, stoned, peeled and chopped into chunks
- 1 small ripe mango, stoned, peeled and chopped into chunks
- 100g spinach (fresh or frozen)
- 250ml vegan milk (unsweetened almond or coconut milk works well)
- 1 tbsp unsweetened almond or peanut butter
- 2 bananas, sliced and frozen
- 1 tbsp agave or maple syrup (optional)

FOR THE SEED MIX
- 1 tbsp chia seeds
- 1 tbsp linseeds
- 4 tbsp pumpkin seeds
- 4 tbsp sunflower seeds
- 4 tbsp coconut flakes
- 4 tbsp flaked almonds
- ¼ tsp ground cinnamon
- 2 tbsp agave or maple syrup

FOR THE TOPPING
- 175g mixed fresh fruit, chopped (we used banana, mango, raspberries and blueberries)

1 For the seed mix, heat oven to 180C/160C fan/gas 4 and line a baking tray with parchment. Tip the seeds, coconut and almonds into a bowl, add the cinnamon and drizzle over the agave or maple syrup. Toss until everything is well coated, then scatter over the baking tray in an even layer. Bake for 10–15 mins, stirring every 5 mins or so, until the seeds are lightly toasted. Leave to cool. Will keep in an airtight container for up to 1 month.

2 Put the avocado, mango, spinach, milk, nut butter, frozen banana slices and agave or maple syrup in a blender and whizz to a thick smoothie consistency – you may have to scrape down the sides with a spoon a few times. Divide between 2 bowls and arrange the fruit on top. Scatter 1–2 tbsp of the seed mix over each bowl and eat straight away.

Nutrition per serving
Kcals 488 · fat 24g · saturates 5g · carbs 52g · sugars 48g · fibre 12g · protein 11g · salt 0.2g

Almond butter

· ·

If you think there's no spread quite like peanut butter, try this version, sweetened with maple syrup, as an energy-boosting snack.

🕐 TAKES 25 mins 🥧 MAKES 1 x 300g jar

- 300g skin-on almonds
- good drizzle maple syrup
- malt loaf or wholegrain bread, to serve (optional)

1 Heat oven to 190C/170C fan/gas 5. Spread the almonds on a baking tray and roast for 10 mins. Remove and allow to cool.
2 Put into a food processor and whizz for 12 mins, stopping every so often to scrape the sides down, and finish with a drizzle of syrup. Serve spread over malt loaf or wholegrain bread. Will keep in the fridge for up to 3 weeks.

· ·

Nutrition (per tbsp)
Kcals 93 • fat 8g • saturates 1g • carbs 1g • sugars 1g • fibre 1g • protein 3g • salt 0g

CHAPTER 2: LUNCHES

A good lunch should see you through the afternoon without needing to reach for the biscuit tin, and these recipes will do just that. Balanced with carbohydrates, fats, protein and plenty of veg, the recipes in this chapter are not only good for you, but are also delicious. Many of them can be packed in a lunchbox or thermos to take to work and often extra portions can be saved for the next day.

Beetroot & avocado nori rolls

The dipping sauce adds real punch to this impressive looking vegan canapé. If you can't get hold of wasabi, substitute for storecupboard horseradish instead.

⏱ TAKES 40 mins ◔ SERVES 15 as canapés or 4 for lunch

FOR THE DIPPING SAUCE
- 1 tsp wasabi
- juice of ½ lime
- 2 tbsp dark soy sauce or tamari
- 1 tsp sesame oil

FOR THE NORI ROLLS
- 1 beetroot (about 120g), peeled, ends trimmed and spiralized into thin noodles
- 3 sheets of nori
- 1 ripe avocado, thinly sliced
- ½ cucumber, ends trimmed, cut in half widthways and spiralized into thin noodles then patted dry to absorb excess moisture
- 2 tsp toasted sesame seeds

1 Mix all of the ingredients for the dipping sauce together in a small bowl then set aside.

2 Cut the spiralized beetroot into thumb-length strips. Lay a nori sheet, shiny side down, onto a sushi rolling mat. Arrange one third of the beetroot, avocado and cucumber in lines across the bottom third of the nori sheet then sprinkle over half the sesame seeds.

3 Rolling away from yourself, lift the edge of the nori over the filling and continue folding to create a roll. When you get to the edge of the nori, dampen with a little water then continue to fold, sealing everything together into a tight roll.

4 Repeat with the remaining nori and filling. Trim the ends of the roll to neaten them then slice into 5 pieces. Serve with the wasabi dipping sauce.

Nutrition per serving
Kcals 32 • fat 2g • saturates 1g • carbs 1g • sugars 1g • fibre 1g • protein 1g • salt 0.3g

Chilli & avocado salsa sweet potatoes

A fresh, summery recipe that won't break the bank. Get 5 of your 5-a-day the easy way.

 TAKES 1 hr ◔ SERVES 2

- 2 large sweet potatoes
- 1 tbsp vegetable oil
- 1 onion, finely chopped
- 2 garlic cloves, crushed
- 1 tsp paprika
- 400g can chopped tomatoes
- 400g can mixed beans, drained
- ½ x 460g jar roasted red peppers, sliced
- 1 tbsp coconut yoghurt, to serve (optional)

FOR THE SALSA
- 1 small avocado, chopped
- 1 red chilli, finely chopped
- ½ small pack coriander, chopped

1 Heat oven to 200C/180C fan/gas 6. Prick the sweet potatoes with a fork and bake for 40–45 mins, or until tender and cooked.
2 Meanwhile, heat the oil in a deep frying pan and cook the onion for about 10 mins until softening. Add the garlic and paprika, and stir for 1 min. Tip in the tomatoes, then bring to a gentle simmer, season well and leave to bubble away for 10–15 mins.
3 To make the salsa, combine the avocado, chilli and coriander in a small bowl. Pour the mixed beans into the pan with the red peppers. Warm through for about 5 mins and taste.
4 Halve each baked potato, ladle over the chilli and spoon on the salsa. Add a dollop of coconut yoghurt to each half before serving, if you like.

Nutrition per serving
Kcals 594 • fat 17g • saturates 3g • carbs 78g • sugars 37g • fibre 24g • protein 18g • salt 0.3g

Sweet potato, peanut butter & chilli quesadillas

Crisp tortillas, soft smoky roasted veg and crunchy nuts give this simple vegan meal lots of texture. An easy iron-rich supper that's full of flavour.

TAKES 1 hr SERVES 2

- 3 medium sweet potatoes, peeled and thinly sliced
- 1 tbsp smoked paprika
- 3 tbsp olive oil, plus extra for brushing
- 1 extra large ripe avocado
- ½ lime, zested and juiced, plus wedges to serve
- 2 tbsp crunchy peanut butter
- 4 small flour tortillas
- sriracha chilli sauce, to taste
- ½ small pack coriander, torn

1 Heat oven to 200C/180C fan/gas 6. Toss the sweet potatoes with the paprika and 2 tbsp olive oil in a roasting tin. Roast for 15 mins, tossing halfway through, until the potatoes are beginning to crisp.

2 Stone, peel and chop the avocado, tip into a bowl with the lime juice and zest, and season generously. Mash together with a fork and set aside. In a small bowl, combine the peanut butter and remaining olive oil. Set aside.

3 Heat a griddle pan or frying pan over a medium heat until very hot. Brush each tortilla on one side with the remaining oil. Place one tortilla, oiled-side down, in the pan and spread over half the peanut butter mixture, half the sweet potatoes, a little chilli sauce and half the coriander. Top with another tortilla, oiled-side up. Press down with a heavy saucepan and cook for 2–3 mins each side until the quesadilla is crisp outside and warm in the middle. Repeat to make a second quesadilla, then cut each into quarters and serve with the crushed avocado and lime wedges.

Nutrition per serving
Kcals 947 • fat 51g • saturates 10g • carbs 96g • sugars 30g • fibre 18g • protein 17g • salt 1.7g

Vegan banh mi

Make this decadent vegan sandwich using veggies and hummus with an Asian dressing and hot sauce all stuffed inside a baguette. Great for a filling lunch.

⏱ TAKES 20 mins 🕐 SERVES 4

- 150g leftover raw veggies, (such as red cabbage and carrots), shredded
- 3 tbsp good-quality vegan white wine vinegar
- 1 tsp golden caster sugar
- 1 long French baguette
- 100g hummus
- 175g cooked tempeh, very finely sliced
- ½ small pack coriander, leaves picked, to serve
- ½ small pack mint, leaves picked, to serve
- hot sauce, to serve (we used sriracha)

1 Put the shredded veg in a bowl and add the vinegar, sugar and 1 tsp salt. Toss everything together, then set aside to pickle quickly while you prepare the rest of the sandwich.

2 Heat oven to 180C/160C fan/gas 4. Cut the baguette into 4, then slice each piece horizontally in half. Put the baguette pieces in the oven for 5 mins until lightly toasted and warm. Spread each piece with a layer of hummus, then top 4 pieces with the tempeh slices and pile the pickled veg on top. To serve, sprinkle over the herbs and squeeze over some hot sauce, then top with the other baguette pieces to make sandwiches.

Nutrition per serving
Kcals 338 • fat 11g • saturates 0g • carbs 40g • sugars 7g • fibre 7g • protein 16g • salt 2.1g

Curried tofu wraps

This spicy vegan supper is big on taste. It's simple to make and packed with chunky tandoori-spiced tofu on a cool mint, yoghurt and red cabbage relish.

🕐 TAKES 45 mins ◗ SERVES 4

- ½ red cabbage (about 500g), shredded
- 4 heaped tbsp dairy-free yoghurt
- 3 tbsp mint sauce
- 3 x 200g packs tofu, each cut into 15 cubes
- 2 tbsp tandoori curry paste
- 2 tbsp oil
- 2 onions, sliced
- 2 large garlic cloves, sliced
- 8 chapatis
- 2 limes, cut into quarters

1 Mix the cabbage, yoghurt and mint sauce, season and set aside. Toss the tofu with the tandoori paste and 1 tbsp of the oil. Heat a frying pan and cook the tofu, in batches, for a few mins each side until golden. Remove from the pan with a slotted spoon and set aside. Add the remaining oil to the pan, stir in the onions and garlic and cook for 8–10 mins until softened. Return the tofu to the pan and season well.

2 Warm the chapatis following pack instructions, then top each one with some cabbage, followed by the curried tofu and a good squeeze of lime.

Nutrition per serving
Kcals 994 • fat 51g • saturates 25g • carbs 73g • sugars 17g • fibre 11g • protein 54g • salt 1.9g

Sweet potato Tex-mex salad

This hearty vegan salad is 4 of your 5-a-day, rich in folate, fibre and vitamin C, plus it has lots of interesting flavours and textures.

 TAKES 40mins SERVES 4

- 600g sweet potatoes, cut into even chunks
- 2 tbsp extra virgin olive oil
- 1 tsp chilli flakes
- 400g can black beans, drained and rinsed
- 198g can sweetcorn, drained and rinsed
- 2 avocados, chopped
- 250g tomatoes, cut into chunks
- 1 small red onion, thinly sliced
- 1 small pack coriander, roughly chopped
- juice 1 lime

1 Heat oven to 200C/180C fan/ gas 6. On a baking tray, toss the sweet potato in 1 tbsp of the oil with the chilli flakes, sea salt and pepper. Roast for 30 mins until tender.
2 Once the sweet potato is nearly ready, combine the remaining ingredients in a large bowl with the remaining 1 tbsp oil and season well. Mix everything well but take care to avoid squashing the avocado. Divide the salad evenly among plates, or serve sharing-style with the sweet potato chunks.

Nutrition per serving
Kcals 485 · fat 21g · saturates 4g · carbs 56g · sugars 27g · fibre 17g · protein 9g · salt 0.6g

Rainbow spring rolls

Try these colourful vegan spring rolls as canapés for a party, vibrant with fresh veg and juicy mango. Serve with a sweet chilli dipping sauce.

🕐 TAKES 30 mins ◔ MAKES 24 rolls

- 12 spring roll wrappers
- ½ small pack mint, leaves picked
- ½ small pack Thai basil, leaves picked (optional)
- 4 spring onions, cut in half then cut lengthways into strips
- 1 courgette, peeled lengthways, halved and cut into thin strips (or use julienne peeler)
- 1 large carrot, halved and cut into thin strips (or use julienne peeler)
- ½ mango, cut into strips
- 1 red chilli, deseeded and cut into thin strips
- 50g salted peanuts, chopped (optional)
- sweet chilli sauce, for dipping

1 Have all your ingredients prepared and ready to go before you start assembling the rolls. Dip a spring roll wrapper into a shallow bowl of water until it just softens (don't leave it too long or you'll be left with a gluey mess). Put the wet wrapper on a chopping board, then top with a couple of mint and basil leaves (if using), and some spring onion, courgette, carrot, mango, chilli and peanuts (if using).
2 Starting with the edge nearest to you, fold the wrapper into the centre so that it covers half the filling. Fold in both of the shorter ends, then, rolling away from you, fold the wrapper over so that the entire filling is encased. Repeat with the remaining wrappers and fillings to make 12 spring rolls. Can be made in the morning and kept in the fridge for later.
3 To serve, cut the spring rolls in half on the diagonal. Serve with sweet chilli dipping sauce on the side.

Nutrition per serving
Kcals 40 • fat 1g • saturates 0g • carbs 6g • sugars 2g • fibre 1g • protein 1g • salt 0.2g

Chickpea curry jacket potato

Get some protein into a vegan diet with this tasty chickpea curry jacket. It's an easy midweek meal, or filling lunch that packs a lot of flavour.

 TAKES 1 hr SERVES 4

- 4 sweet potatoes
- 1 tbsp coconut oil
- 1½ tsp cumin seeds
- 1 large onion, diced
- 2 garlic cloves, crushed
- thumb-sized piece ginger, finely grated
- 1 green chilli, finely chopped
- 1 tsp garam masala
- 1 tsp ground coriander
- ½ tsp turmeric
- 2 tbsp tikka masala paste
- 2 x 400g cans chopped tomatoes
- 2 x 400g cans chickpeas, drained
- lemon wedges and coriander leaves, to serve

1 Heat oven to 200C/180C fan/gas 6. Prick the sweet potatoes all over with a fork, then put on a baking tray and roast in the oven for 45 mins or until tender when pierced with a knife.

2 Meanwhile, melt the coconut oil in a large saucepan over a medium heat. Add the cumin seeds and fry for 1 min until fragrant, then add the onion and fry for 7–10 mins until softened.

3 Put the garlic, ginger and green chilli into the pan, and cook for 2–3 mins. Add the spices and tikka masala paste and cook for a further 2 mins until fragrant, then tip in the tomatoes. Bring to a simmer, then tip in the chickpeas and cook for a further 20 mins until thickened. Season.

4 Put the roasted sweet potatoes on 4 plates and cut open lengthways. Spoon over the chickpea curry and squeeze over the lemon wedges. Season, then scatter with coriander before serving.

Nutrition per serving
Kcals 276 • fat 9g • saturates 3g • carbs 32g • sugars 12g • fibre 11g • protein 12g • salt 0.3g

Curried squash, lentil & coconut soup

Flavour up butternut squash with Indian spices for this warming and healthy soup.

 TAKES 35 mins SERVES 6

- 1 tbsp olive oil
- 1 butternut squash, peeled, deseeded and diced
- 200g carrot, diced
- 1 tbsp curry powder containing turmeric
- 100g red lentils
- 700ml low-sodium vegetable stock
- 400ml can reduced-fat coconut milk
- coriander and naan bread, to serve

1 Heat the oil in a large saucepan, add the squash and carrots, sizzle for 1 min, then stir in the curry powder and cook for 1 min more. Tip in the lentils, the vegetable stock and coconut milk and give everything a good stir. Bring to the boil, then turn the heat down and simmer for 15–18 mins until everything is tender.
2 Using a hand blender or in a food processor, blitz until the soup is as smooth as you like. Taste and season and serve scattered with roughly chopped coriander and some naan bread alongside.

Nutrition per serving
Kcals 178 • fat 7g • saturates 5g • carbs 22g • sugars 9g • fibre 4g • protein 6g • salt 0.4g

Luxury hummus

Use good-quality giant chickpeas to give this vegan hummus a really silky feel. Dips make perfect, easy party food to serve with crudités and warm pittas.

⏱ TAKES 25 mins ◔ SERVES 8

- 700g jar giant chickpeas, drained
- 135ml extra virgin olive oil, plus extra for drizzling
- 2 garlic cloves, roughly chopped
- 1 tbsp tahini
- 1½ lemons, juiced

FOR THE TOPPINGS
- ½ tsp smoked paprika
- ½ tsp sumac
- ½ small pack parsley, roughly chopped
- 40g pomegranate seeds
- crudités and warm pittas, to serve

1 Blitz ¾ of the chickpeas and 120ml of the oil with the rest of the hummus ingredients and a good amount of seasoning in a food processor. Add a little water if it is too thick. Spoon the hummus into a serving bowl or spread it onto a plate. The hummus can be made up to 2 days in advance and kept in the fridge.

2 Dry the rest of the chickpeas on kitchen paper as much as possible. Heat the remaining oil in a frying pan over a medium heat. Add the chickpeas and a large pinch of salt, and fry until golden, around 4 mins. Drain on kitchen paper.

3 Drizzle some oil over the hummus, then sprinkle with the spices, parsley and pomegranate seeds. Scatter the fried chickpeas on top and serve with crudités and warm pitta breads.

Nutrition per serving
Kcals 242 • fat 20g • saturates 3g • carbs 10g • sugars 1g • fibre 4g • protein 5g • salt 0.4g

No cook festival burrito

This vegan wrap doesn't require any cooking, just lashings of lime and chilli sauce for delicious festival or camping sustenance.

TAKES 30 mins   SERVES 4

- 100g bulgur wheat
- 120g cherry tomatoes
- 4 tortilla wraps
- 215g can kidney beans, drained
- 198g can sweetcorn, drained
- 200g smoked tofu
- 50g grilled red peppers
- 1 avocado, roughly chopped
- 3 tbsp tahini
- 1 lime, quartered
- chilli sauce, to serve (optional)

1 Put the bulgur wheat into a bowl and add 100ml of boiling water. Cover and leave to soak for 35–40 mins.
2 Put the cherry tomatoes into a food bag. Holding the end of the bag closed loosely with one had squish the tomatoes through the bag with the other – like popping bubble wrap. This should separate the juice from the rest of the tomatoes without making a mess or needing a knife and chopping board. Carefully pour the tomato juice into the bowl of bulgur wheat, reserving the tomato pieces inside the bag for later.
3 When the bulgur wheat has finished soaking, give it a stir and season with salt and pepper. In a small bowl or cup mix the tahini with 3 tbsp of water to make a smooth, pourable sauce then set aside.
4 Lay the tortilla wraps out onto a big board or onto 4 plates and divide the bulgur wheat, kidney beans and sweetcorn between them (try to keep the filling in the middle). Crumble the smoked tofu over the top then add the crushed tomatoes, grilled peppers, avocado pieces and a good drizzle of the tahini sauce, a squeeze of lime and some chilli sauce, if you like.
5 Fold the right and left sides of the wrap in to the middle first and then roll the bottom all the way over to completely enclose the filling inside each wrap, push down to seal. Serve immediately with extra lime and chilli sauce on the side.

Nutrition per burrito
Kcals 524 • fat 24g • saturates 5g • carbs 47g • sugars 5g • fibre 13g • protein 23g • salt 1.5g

Beetroot hummus & crispy chickpea sub sandwich

Load up a sub with homemade hummus, beetroot, chickpeas and salad to make this filling vegan sandwich. An ideal lunch for when hunger strikes.

 TAKES 20 mins SERVES 2

- 300g pack cooked beetroot in water, drained, half sliced
- 400g can chickpeas, drained
- 3 tbsp vegetarian pesto
- olive oil
- splash of vinegar (white wine vinegar if you have it)
- 2 large ciabatta rolls, sliced in half
- 2 large handfuls mixed rocket, watercress & spinach salad

1 Blitz the whole beetroot, ¾ of the chickpeas, 2 tbsp pesto and 1 tbsp oil in a food processor with some seasoning until you have a thick, smooth hummus. Heat the ciabatta following the pack instructions.

2 Fry the remaining chickpeas in a little oil until crisp, then set aside. Toss the salad leaves with the remaining pesto and a splash of vinegar. Slice the rolls, then assemble the sandwiches with the hummus, beetroot slices, salad leaves and fried chickpeas.

Nutrition per serving
Kcals 639 • fat 22g • saturates 3g • carbs 77g • sugars 16g • fibre 14g • protein 24g • salt 1.6g

Roasted cauli-broc bowl with tahini hummus

A simple quinoa bowl you can assemble in 10 minutes and enjoy al-desko. It's vegan, healthy and gluten-free.

🕐 TAKES 40 mins 🍕 SERVES 2

- 400g pack cauliflower & broccoli florets
- 2 tbsp olive oil
- 250g ready-to-eat quinoa
- 2 cooked beetroots, sliced
- large handful baby spinach
- 10 walnuts, toasted and chopped
- 2 tbsp tahini
- 3 tbsp hummus
- 1 lemon, ½ juiced, ½ cut into wedges

1 The night before, heat oven to 200C/180C fan/gas 6. Put the cauliflower and broccoli in a large roasting tin with the oil and a sprinkle of flaky sea salt. Roast for 25–30 mins until browned and cooked. Leave to cool completely.

2 Build each bowl by putting half the quinoa in each. Lay the slices of beetroot on top, followed by the spinach, cauliflower, broccoli and walnuts. Combine the tahini, hummus, lemon juice and 1 tbsp water in a small pot. Before eating, coat in the dressing. Serve the bowl with the lemon wedges.

Nutrition per serving
Kcals 533 · fat 37g · saturates 4g · carbs 28g · sugars 6g · fibre 10g · protein 16g · salt 0.8g

Mushroom & potato soup

Porcini mushrooms give this healthy soup a real umami flavour boost. Pour into a flask for a warming, low-calorie lunch that you can take to work.

TAKES 45 mins   SERVES 4

- 1 tbsp rapeseed oil
- 2 large onions, halved and thinly sliced
- 20g dried porcini mushrooms
- 3 tsp vegetable bouillon powder
- 300g chestnut mushrooms, chopped
- 3 garlic cloves, finely grated
- 300g potato, finely diced
- 2 tsp fresh thyme
- 4 carrots, finely diced
- 2 tbsp chopped parsley, plus extra to sprinkle
- 8 tbsp dairy-free yoghurt
- 55g walnut pieces

1 Heat the oil in a large pan. Tip in the onions and fry for 10 mins until golden. Meanwhile, pour 1.2 litres boiling water over the dried mushrooms and stir in the bouillon.

2 Add the fresh mushrooms and garlic to the pan with the potatoes, thyme and carrots, and continue to fry until the mushrooms soften and start to brown.

3 Pour in the dried mushrooms and stock, cover the pan and leave to simmer for 20 mins. Stir in the parsley and plenty of pepper. Ladle into bowls and serve each portion topped with 2 tbsp yoghurt, a quarter of the walnuts and extra parsley. The rest can be chilled and reheated the next day.

Nutrition per serving
Kcals 315 • fat 15g • saturates 2g • carbs 33g • sugars 17g • fibre 9g • protein 12g • salt 0.3g

Veggie olive wraps with mustard vinaigrette

Eat the rainbow with our simple, healthy, veggie wrap. This olive and veg sandwich makes an easy vegan, low-calorie lunch option to eat al-desko.

 TAKES 10 mins SERVES 1

- 1 carrot, shredded or coarsely grated
- 80g wedge red cabbage, finely shredded
- 2 spring onions, thinly sliced
- 1 courgette, shredded or coarsely grated
- handful basil leaves
- 5 green olives, pitted and halved
- ½ tsp English mustard powder
- 2 tsp extra virgin rapeseed oil
- 1 tbsp cider vinegar
- 1 large seeded tortilla

1 Mix all the ingredients except for the tortilla and toss well.
2 Put the tortilla on a sheet of foil and pile the filling along one side of the wrap – it will almost look like too much mixture, but once you start to roll it firmly it will compact. Roll the tortilla from the filling side, folding in the sides as you go. Fold the foil in at the ends to keep stuff inside the wrap.
3 Cut in half and eat straight away. If taking to work, leave whole and wrap up like a cracker in baking parchment.

Nutrition per serving
Kcals 281 • fat 12g • saturates 2g • carbs 31g • sugars 12g • fibre 10g • protein 8g • salt 0.9g

Roast asparagus bowls with tahini lemon dressing

Enjoy 5 of your 5-a-day with this dish, a tasty mix of asparagus, quinoa, aduki beans, onion and cherry tomatoes. It's packed with nutrients.

 TAKES 40 mins ⦿ SERVES 2

- 2 red onions, halved and thickly sliced
- 2 tsp rapeseed oil
- 250g pack asparagus, woody ends trimmed
- 160g cherry tomatoes
- 2 tbsp sunflower seeds
- 1 tsp vegetable bouillon powder
- 120g quinoa
- 2 tsp tahini
- ½ lemon, juiced
- 1 large garlic clove, finely grated
- 2 tsp tamari
- 2 good handfuls rocket
- 400g aduki beans in water, drained

1 Heat oven to 220C/200C fan/gas 7. Toss the onions in 1 tsp rapeseed oil and roast on a baking sheet for 10 mins. Coat the asparagus with the remaining oil and spread over another sheet. After 10 mins, add the asparagus to roast with the onions for 5 mins. Add the tomatoes and sunflower seeds and roast for 5 mins. The onions should be charred, the asparagus tender, the seeds toasted and the whole tomatoes near bursting.

2 Meanwhile, tip the bouillon and quinoa into a pan. Add 360ml water, cover and simmer for 20 mins until tender and the water has been absorbed. Whisk the tahini and lemon juice with 3 tbsp warm water, the garlic and tamari to make a dressing.

3 Pile the quinoa into bowls, top with rocket, spoon over half the dressing, add a pile of beans with the tomatoes, then a separate pile of the asparagus and onions. Spoon over the remaining dressing and scatter over the sunflower seeds. Will keep in the fridge for 2 days.

Nutrition per serving
Kcals 583 • fat 18g • saturates 2g • carbs 66g • sugars 17g • fibre 21g • protein 28g • salt 0.9g

Crunchy bulgur salad

A vibrant summer salad with radishes, edamame beans, peppers, almonds and fresh herbs, drizzled with a tangy citrus dressing.

 TAKES 25 mins SERVES 4

- 200g bulgur wheat
- 150g frozen podded edamame (soya) beans
- 2 Romano peppers, sliced into rounds, seeds removed
- 150g radishes, finely sliced
- 75g whole blanched almonds
- small bunch mint, finely chopped
- small bunch parsley, finely chopped
- 2 oranges
- 3 tbsp extra virgin olive oil

1 Cook the bulgur following pack instructions, then drain and tip into a large serving bowl to cool. Meanwhile, put the edamame beans in a small bowl, pour over boiling water, leave for 1 min, then drain. Put in a serving bowl with the peppers, radishes, almonds, mint and parsley.

2 Peel 1 orange, carefully cut away the segments and add to the bowl. Squeeze the juice of the other into a jam jar with the oil. Season well and shake to emulsify. Pour over the salad, toss well and serve.

Nutrition per serving
Kcals 483 • fat 22g • saturates 2g • carbs 50g • sugars 11g • fibre 9g • protein 17g • salt 0g

Celeriac, hazelnut & truffle soup

Rustle up this healthy vegan celeriac and hazelnut soup as a starter. Truffle oil adds a bit of luxury, or leave it out for a simple supper on a winter's night.

🕐 TAKES 1 hr 5 mins ⏳ SERVES 6

- 1 tbsp olive oil
- small bunch thyme
- 2 bay leaves
- 1 onion, chopped
- 1 fat garlic clove, chopped
- 1 celeriac (about 1kg), peeled and chopped
- 1 potato (about 200g), chopped
- 1 litre veg stock (check the label to ensure it's vegan)
- 100ml soya cream
- 1 tbsp truffle oil, plus an extra drizzle to serve
- 50g blanched hazelnuts, toasted and roughly chopped

1 In a large saucepan, heat the oil over a low heat. Tie the thyme sprigs and bay leaves together with a piece of string and add them to the pan with the onion and a pinch of salt. Cook for about 10 mins until softened but not coloured.

2 Stir in the garlic and cook for 1 min more, then tip in the celeriac and potato. Give everything a good stir and season with a big pinch of salt and white pepper. Pour in the stock, bring to the boil, then simmer for around 30 mins until the vegetables are completely soft.

3 Discard the herbs, then stir through the cream, remove from the heat and blitz until completely smooth. Stir through ½ tbsp truffle oil at a time and taste for seasoning – the strength of the oil will vary, so it's better to start with less oil and add a little at a time.

4 To serve, reheat the soup until piping hot, then ladle into bowls and top with the hazelnuts, some black pepper and an extra drizzle of truffle oil.

Nutrition per serving
Kcals 237 • fat 15g • saturates 2g • carbs 14g • sugars 5g • fibre 11g • protein 5g • salt 0.6g

Tomato bruschetta

Make our simple tomato bruschetta as a classic Italian starter. Ideal for a summer gathering with friends, this easy dish is fresh, tasty and full of flavour.

🕐 TAKES 20 mins plus 1 hour marinating ⏲ SERVES 12

- ½ small red onion, finely chopped
- 8 medium tomatoes (about 500g), coarsely chopped and drained
- 2–3 garlic cloves, crushed
- 6–8 leaves of fresh basil, finely chopped
- 30ml balsamic vinegar
- 60–80ml extra virgin olive oil
- 1 loaf crusty bread

1 In a large bowl, mix the onion, tomatoes, garlic and basil, taking care not to mash or break up the tomatoes too much. Add the balsamic vinegar and extra virgin olive oil. Add salt and pepper to taste. Mix again. Cover and chill for at least an hour. This will allow the flavours to soak and blend together.

2 Slice the baguette loaf diagonally into 12 thick slices and lightly toast them until they are light brown on both sides. Serve the mixture on the warm slices of bread. If you prefer the mixture at room temperature, remove from the fridge half an hour before serving.

Nutrition per serving
Kcals 310 • fat 12g • saturates 2g • carbs 42g • sugars 6g • fibre 3g • protein 8g • salt 0.72g

Curried cashew dip

Just blitz cashews, coconut and curry spices for an easy dip that's perfect for any party table. Serve with crudités or fluffy naan bread.

🕐 TAKES 5 mins 🕒 SERVES 4

- 100g cashew nuts
- juice of 1–2 limes
- 3 tbsp coconut cream
- 2 tbsp korma curry paste
- 2 tbsp Bombay spice mix

TO SERVE
- carrot sticks and naan bread

1 Tip all the ingredients, except the Bombay mix, into a food processor. Blend until smooth, then season to taste. If the mixture is too thick, add a little more lime juice or a splash of cold water.

2 Spoon into a bowl and sprinkle over the Bombay mix before serving with carrot sticks and naan bread.

Nutrition per serving
Kcals 315 • fat 26g • saturates 12g • carbs 9g • sugars 4g • fibre 2g • protein 8g • salt 0.4g

Cashew cream cheese

Nothing beats a herby cream cheese. Have this dairy-free spread on toast or stir it into a pasta dish. Our vegan version is easy to make and there's no cooking involved.

TAKES 15 mins plus soaking and chilling · MAKES about 400g

- 250g cashews
- 2 tbsp nutritional yeast
- juice 1 lemon
- a few chives, chopped (optional)

1 Place the cashews in a large bowl and cover with water. Cover the bowl with cling film and leave to soak overnight or for at least 4 hrs.

2 Drain and rinse the cashews then add them to a food processor with the nutritional yeast, lemon juice, ½ tsp salt and 1 tbsp water. Whizz until very smooth, about 5 mins. You may need to stop and scrape the sides down with a spatula.

3 Transfer the cashew cheese to a dish or bowl and stir through the chives, if using. Cover with cling film and place in the fridge for 1 hr to firm up a little. The cheese will keep in the fridge for up to 3–4 days.

Nutrition per tbsp
Kcals 124 · fat 9g · saturates 2g · carbs 4g · sugars 1g · fibre 1g · protein 5g · salt 0.3g

CHAPTER 3: MIDWEEK MEALS

Midweek meals should be quick and easy to prepare with minimal ingredients, and eating a vegan diet shouldn't change that. The recipes in this chapter can all be on the table in an hour or less and will be loved by the whole family.

Coconut curry noodle bowl

This creamy noodle dish is topped with crunchy cashew nuts for added flavour and texture. It's a simple vegan supper, perfect for feeding the family.

 TAKES 35 mins SERVES 4

FOR THE SAUCE
- 1 tbsp vegetable oil
- 2 garlic cloves, crushed
- ½ red chilli, finely chopped (optional)
- small piece ginger, grated
- 1 tbsp mild curry powder
- 1 tbsp soy sauce
- 1 tbsp sriracha (or another 1 tbsp soy sauce if you don't want the sauce hot)
- 400g can coconut milk

FOR THE NUTS
- 80g cashew nuts
- 1 tsp soy sauce
- 1 tsp maple syrup

FOR THE STIR-FRY
- 1 tsp sesame oil
- 2 heads pak choi, halved
- 200g green beans, trimmed and halved
- 2 carrots, peeled into long ribbons
- 3 x 150g packs fresh udon noodles
- large handful coriander, chopped, to serve

1 Heat the oil in a large saucepan, add the garlic, chilli (if using) and ginger, and fry on a low heat for about 5 mins until softened. Add the curry powder and stir, frying for 1 min more until aromatic. Add the soy sauce and sriracha (if using), and stir again. Pour in the coconut milk, breaking up any solids on the top of the can with a spoon. Stir until combined, then leave the sauce on a medium heat with a lid on to simmer for 15 mins.

2 Meanwhile, heat oven to 200C/180C fan/gas 6. Put the nuts in a bowl and mix with the soy sauce and maple syrup until fully coated. Scatter the nuts on a sheet of baking parchment on a baking tray, and roast for 10–12 mins, stirring halfway through.

3 While the nuts are roasting, heat the sesame oil in a wok or large frying pan. When hot, add the veg and stir-fry for 3–4 mins until slightly softened. Add the noodles and fry for another 2 mins until heated through.

4 Take both pans off the heat and pour the coconut sauce into the wok (or add the noodles to the saucepan) and stir until everything is coated in the sauce. Spoon into bowls and scatter over the nuts and coriander.

Nutrition per serving
Kcals 533 • fat 31g • saturates 17g • carbs 44g • sugars 11g • fibre 10g • protein 15g • salt 1.3g

Artichoke & aubergine rice

As well as being tasty, this aubergine and artichoke dish is low-fat, low-calorie and cost effective. Make a large batch and eat it cold the next day.

⏱ TAKES 1 hr 5 mins 🥧 SERVES 6

- 60ml olive oil
- 2 aubergines, cut into chunks
- 1 large onion, finely chopped
- 2 garlic cloves, crushed
- small pack parsley, leaves picked, stalks finely chopped
- 2 tsp smoked paprika
- 2 tsp turmeric
- 400g paella rice
- 1½ litres vegetable stock
- 2 x 175g packs chargrilled artichokes
- 2 lemons, 1 juiced, 1 cut into wedges to serve

1 Heat 2 tbsp of the oil in a large non-stick frying pan or paella pan. Fry the aubergines until nicely coloured on all sides (add another tbsp of oil if the aubergine begins catching too much), then remove and set aside. Add another tbsp of oil to the pan and lightly fry the onion for 2–3 mins or until softened. Add the garlic and parsley stalks, cook for a few mins more, then stir in the spices and rice until everything is well coated. Heat for 2 mins, add half the stock and cook, uncovered, over a medium heat for 20 mins, stirring occasionally to prevent it from sticking.

2 Nestle the aubergine and artichokes into the mixture, pour over the rest of the stock and cook for 20 mins more or until the rice is cooked through. Chop the parsley leaves, stir through with the lemon juice and season well. Bring the whole pan to the table and spoon into bowls, with the lemon wedges on the side.

Nutrition per serving
Kcals 431 • fat 16g • saturates 2g • carbs 58g • sugars 9g • fibre 11g • protein 8g • salt 1.5g

Dhal with garam masala carrots

If you're looking for a budget meal for one, look no further than this delicious dhal topped with spicy carrots. It's healthy and low-calorie too.

⏱ TAKES 25 mins ◔ SERVES 1

- 75g red lentils
- 1 garlic clove, peeled
- 2 carrots, cut into batons
- 1 tbsp rapeseed oil
- ½ tsp garam masala
- 1 tsp nigella seeds (kalonji) (optional)
- 1 tsp soya or coconut yoghurt

1 Cook the lentils in 500ml water with the garlic clove for around 20 mins until the lentils are tender. Fish the garlic clove out, crush it and stir it back into the lentils. Season well. It should be spoonable like a thick soup – keep simmering if it's not thick enough.

2 Put the carrots in a pan, just cover with water, bring to the boil and simmer until just tender, about 8–10 mins. Drain, then toss in the oil and garam masala. Tip into a frying pan and fry until the carrots start to brown, then add the nigella seeds, if using, and fry for another min.

3 Serve the dhal in a bowl with the yoghurt and carrots, with the remaining spices and oil from the pan on top.

Nutrition per serving
Kcals 475 • fat 19g • saturates 4g • carbs 51g • sugars 10g • fibre 10g • protein 20g • salt 0.3g

Grilled aubergine tabbouleh

A vegan tabbouleh with all the flavours of summer. The coconut and tahini dressing adds a creamy, nutty element to this winning couscous.

 TAKES 25 mins SERVES 2

- 2 tbsp garlic-infused oil
- 1 large aubergine, diced
- 160g couscous
- ½ cucumber, diced
- 200g cherry tomatoes, halved
- small pack mint, roughly chopped
- small pack parsley, roughly chopped

FOR THE DRESSING
- juice 1 lemon
- 5 tbsp coconut yoghurt
- 2 tbsp tahini
- 1 tbsp maple syrup

1 Heat the oil in a frying pan over a medium-high heat and add the aubergine. Cook for 10 mins until soft and cooked through.
2 Meanwhile, put the couscous in a large bowl and pour over 200ml boiling water. Cover with cling film and leave to stand for 5–6 mins.
3 Combine all the ingredients for the dressing and season to taste.
4 When the couscous has absorbed all the water, fluff it up with a fork.
5 Season and stir in the cucumber, tomatoes and herbs. Add half the dressing and toss to coat. Scatter over the aubergine and drizzle over the rest of the dressing to serve.

Nutrition per serving
Kcals 630 • fat 33g • saturates 10g • carbs 58g • sugars 18g • fibre 14g • protein 17g • salt 0.1g

Veggie protein chilli

· ·

A protein-packed vegan chilli, perfect after a run or gym workout. This easy supper is simple to make and freezable if you want to batch cook.

🕐 TAKES 1 hr 10 mins 🕐 SERVES 2

- 1 tbsp olive oil
- ½ onion, finely chopped
- ½ red chilli, finely chopped
- 1 garlic clove, finely chopped
- 1 small sweet potato, peeled and cut into chunks
- ½ tsp cumin
- ½ tsp paprika
- ½ tsp cayenne pepper
- ½ tsp cinnamon
- 400g can mixed beans
- 400g can chopped tomatoes
- 1 lime, juiced, to serve
- cauliflower rice, to serve

1 Heat the oil in a large saucepan and add the onion, chilli and garlic and cook without colouring for 1–2 mins. Tip in the sweet potato, spices and some seasoning, then pour in the beans and chopped tomatoes. Fill one of the empty cans with water and add to the pan, then bring to the boil and turn down to a simmer.

2 Cook for 45–50 mins or until the sweet potato is soft and the sauce has reduced – add some water if the sauce looks a bit thick. Stir through the lime juice, season to taste and serve with cauliflower rice.

· ·

Nutrition per serving
Kcals 658 · fat 17g · saturates 2g · carbs 88g · sugars 32g · fibre 23g · protein 25g · salt 1.1g

Garlicky mushroom penne

Add protein to a vegan pasta dish by using a low-fat hummus in the sauce. With the mushrooms and wholemeal penne, you have a healthy and filling dinner.

TAKES 35 mins SERVES 2

- 210g can chickpeas, no need to drain
- 1 tbsp lemon juice
- 1 large garlic clove
- 1 tsp vegetable bouillon
- 2 tsp tahini
- ¼ tsp ground coriander
- 115g wholemeal penne
- 2 tsp rapeseed oil
- 2 red onions, halved and sliced
- 200g closed cup mushrooms, roughly chopped
- generous handful chopped parsley
- ½ lemon, juiced

1 To make the hummus, tip the chickpeas and their liquid into a bowl and add the lemon juice, garlic, bouillon, tahini and ground coriander. Blitz to a wet paste with a hand blender, still retaining some texture from the chickpeas.
2 Cook the pasta according to pack instructions. Meanwhile, heat the oil in a non-stick wok or large frying pan and add the onions and mushrooms, stirring frequently until softened and starting to caramelise.
3 Drain the pasta and tip in with the mushrooms, then take off the heat and stir through the hummus and parsley. Toss together lightly, squeeze over the lemon juice and serve, adding a dash of water to loosen the mixture a little if needed.

Nutrition per serving
Kcals 436 • fat 12g • saturates 1g • carbs 59g • sugars 11g • fibre 13g • protein 18g • salt 0.2g

Roasted aloo gobi

This extra special curry uses roasted cauliflower and potatoes for extra flavour. You can also serve as a side to other curries.

TAKES 1 hr 5 mins SERVES 4

- 400g floury potatoes (such as Maris Piper or King Edward), cut into medium-sized chunks
- 1 large cauliflower, cut into florets
- 1 tbsp cumin seeds, lightly crushed
- 2 tsp coriander seeds, lightly crushed
- 2 tsp nigella seeds
- 1 tsp ground cinnamon
- 1 tsp turmeric
- 1 tsp chilli powder
- 4 tbsp vegetable, sunflower or rapeseed oil
- 8 curry leaves
- 4 garlic cloves, crushed
- 2 x 400g cans chopped tomatoes
- 2 small green chillies, pierced a few times
- 1 tsp golden caster sugar
- 1 lime, juiced
- small pack coriander, chopped
- basmati rice, naan and coconut yoghurt, to serve

1 Heat oven to 180C/160C fan/gas 4. Tip the potatoes into a large pan, fill with cold water and bring to the boil. Simmer for 5–6 mins until starting to soften but still holding their shape. Drain well.

2 On a large baking tray, toss the potatoes and cauliflower with the spices and 2 tbsp oil. Season well and roast for 45 mins, stirring halfway through cooking, until the veg is soft and starting to brown.

3 Meanwhile, heat the remaining oil in a large pan. Fry the curry leaves and garlic for 1 min, making sure the garlic doesn't brown. Add the tomatoes, chillies, sugar, lime juice and some seasoning. Cover with a lid and simmer for 15 mins until the tomatoes have broken down.

4 Add the roasted veg to the sauce. Simmer for 5 mins, adding a splash of water if the curry gets too thick. Stir through the coriander and serve with rice, warm naan and yoghurt.

Nutrition per serving
Kcals 322 • fat 15g • saturates 1g • carbs 33g • sugars 14g • fibre 9g • protein 10g • salt 0.1g

Pea falafels with minty couscous salad

Give falafel a makeover by using a mix of chickpeas and frozen peas. Serve with couscous and a dollop of yoghurt for a cheap but tasty meal.

 TAKES 35 mins SERVES 4

- 400g frozen peas
- 400g can chickpeas, drained
- 3 tbsp flour, plus a little for dusting
- 2 garlic cloves, crushed
- 2 tsp cumin seeds
- 2 tbsp smooth peanut butter or tahini
- small bunch parsley, chopped
- zest and juice of 1 lemon
- 200g couscous
- 3 tbsp olive oil
- small bunch mint, chopped
- 4 large tomatoes, chopped
- 100ml soya or coconut yoghurt

1 Put the peas in a colander and run under the hot tap to defrost. Drain well, then put half into a food processor. Add the chickpeas, flour, garlic, cumin seeds, peanut butter or tahini, parsley, lemon zest and plenty of seasoning. Whizz the ingredients to a paste, adding a splash of water if it looks too crumbly. Using wet hands, shape the mixture into 8 patties, dust with flour, then place on a plate and chill for 10 mins, or longer if you have time. Boil the kettle.

2 Place the couscous in a large bowl, season, then pour over enough boiling water to just cover. Set aside for 5 mins.

3 Heat 2 tbsp oil in a large pan. Cook the falafels for 2–3 mins on each side, until crisp and golden – you may have to do this in batches, so keep them warm in a low oven while you do. Add the remaining oil, lemon juice, mint, tomatoes and peas to the couscous. Serve the salad and falafels with a dollop of yoghurt.

Nutrition per serving
Kcals 489 • fat 17g • saturates 3g • carbs 57g • sugars 8g • fibre 14g • protein 21g • salt 0.5g

Baked ratatouille with lemon breadcrumbs

The staple vegetarian dish is spruced up with a citrussy sourdough crust – chunkily chop your courgettes, onion, peppers and tomatoes for extra texture.

 TAKES 40 mins SERVES 4

- 50g fresh sourdough breadcrumbs
- 3 tbsp extra virgin olive oil
- 3 courgettes, chunkily sliced
- 1 red pepper, cut into chunks
- 1 yellow pepper, cut into chunks
- 1 large onion, very roughly chopped
- 4 ripe plum tomatoes, cut into chunks
- 2 garlic cloves, sliced
- 1 tbsp chopped thyme
- 1 tbsp tomato purée
- 2 tbsp white wine vinegar
- zest 1 lemon

1 Heat oven to 190C/170C fan/gas 5. In a small bowl, toss the breadcrumbs with 2 tbsp of the oil and a good sprinkling of seasoning. Set aside.

2 Put the courgettes, peppers, onion, tomatoes, garlic, thyme, tomato purée, vinegar and the remaining olive oil in a bowl. Season well and toss together. Tip the vegetables into a roasting tin and spread out in a single layer. Cover with foil and bake for 20 mins. Remove the foil. Sprinkle the breadcrumbs on top and bake for another 10 mins or until golden. Remove from the oven and sprinkle over the lemon zest.

Nutrition per serving
Kcals 188 • fat 9g • saturates 1g • carbs 20g • sugars 12g • fibre 6g • protein 5g • salt 0.4g

Miso roasted tofu with sweet potato

A blend of miso and mirin give this extra-special tofu dish added depth of flavour. This simple vegan main course is flavourful, fresh and filling.

🕐 TAKES 45 mins 🕐 SERVES 2

- 400g firm tofu, drained
- 100g fine green beans
- 2 tbsp vegetable oil
- 2 tbsp black or white sesame seeds, toasted
- 2 large sweet potatoes
- 2 spring onions, finely sliced

FOR THE DRESSING
- 3 tbsp white miso (if you can't find it, use 2 tbsp brown miso paste)
- 3 tbsp mirin
- 3 tbsp lime juice

1 Heat oven to 200C/180C fan/gas 6. Wrap the tofu in kitchen paper, place in a shallow dish and put a heavy plate on top to help squeeze out the water. When the paper is wet, replace with another wrapping and weigh down again. Chop the tofu into medium cubes (about 2.5cm). In a small bowl, mix the dressing together with a whisk.

2 Boil the beans for 1 min, then drain, rinse in cold water and set aside. Line a baking tray with parchment, spread out the tofu and pour over half the dressing. Sprinkle the sesame seeds on top and mix well. Bake for 20–25 mins until golden and crisp. Meanwhile, cut the sweet potatoes in half, place in a bowl, cover with cling film and microwave for 10–15 mins until very soft.

3 Mash the sweet potato and serve in bowls with the tofu, green beans, the dressing poured over and some spring onions sprinkled on top.

Nutrition per serving
Kcals 628 • fat 24g • saturates 4g • carbs 72g • sugars 41g • fibre 12g • protein 25g • salt 0.2g

Veggie tahini lentils

Quick, easy and packed with healthy veg, this is a great midweek meal for vegans and veggies.

⏱ TAKES 20 mins ◔ SERVES 4

- 50g tahini
- zest and juice 1 lemon
- 2 tbsp olive oil
- 1 red onion, thinly sliced
- 1 garlic clove, crushed
- 1 yellow pepper, thinly sliced
- 200g green beans, trimmed and halved
- 1 courgette, sliced into half moons
- 100g shredded kale
- 250g pack pre-cooked Puy lentils

1 In a jug, mix the tahini with the zest and juice of the lemon and 50ml of cold water to make a runny dressing. Season to taste, then set aside.

2 Heat the oil in a wok or large frying pan over a medium-high heat. Add the red onion, along with a pinch of salt, and fry for 2 mins until starting to soften and colour. Add the garlic, pepper, green beans and courgette and fry for 5 min, stirring frequently.

3 Tip in the kale, lentils and the tahini dressing. Keep the pan on the heat for a couple of mins, stirring everything together until the kale is wilted and it's all coated in the creamy dressing.

Nutrition per serving
Kcals 293 • fat 14g • saturates 2g • carbs 23g • sugars 7g • fibre 10g • protein 13g • salt 0.7g

Satay tofu skewers with garlic & ginger pak choi

Stay full for longer with these protein-packed satay skewers served with pak choi and peanuts. They make a tasty vegan supper in just 25 minutes.

🕐 TAKES 25 mins SERVES 2

- 3 tbsp smooth peanut butter
- 1 tsp light soy sauce
- pinch of chilli flakes
- 1 lime, ½ juiced, ½ cut into wedges
- 200g firm tofu, cut into chunks
- 1 tbsp rapeseed oil
- 1 garlic clove, sliced
- small piece of ginger, sliced
- 200g pak choi, leaves separated
- 1 tbsp roasted peanuts

YOU WILL NEED
- 4 skewers (soak in cold water for 20 mins if they're wooden)

1 Mix the peanut butter, soy, chilli and lime juice together with 50ml water. Pour half into a roasting tin, add the chunks of tofu and stir to coat. Leave to marinate for 30 mins if you have time, then thread onto 4 skewers and put on a baking tray.

2 Heat the grill to its highest setting. Grill the tofu for 4 mins on each side until nicely browned and crisp. Meanwhile, heat the oil in a frying pan or wok. Add the garlic and ginger and sizzle for 1 min or so, then tip in the pak choi and cook for about 3 mins until wilted.

3 Divide the pak choi and skewers between the plates. Sprinkle over the peanuts, drizzle over the remaining sauce and serve with lime wedges for squeezing over.

Nutrition per serving
Kcals 339 • fat 25g • saturates 5g • carbs 8g • sugars 4g • fibre 5g • protein 18g • salt 0.8g

Vegan BBQ teriyaki tofu

Serve this easy vegan teriyaki dish at a summer barbecue. Allow the tofu to soak up the delicious flavours of the marinade before placing on the coals.

TAKES 25 mins plus 1 hr chilling SERVES 4

- 4 tbsp low-salt soy sauce
- 2 tbsp soft brown sugar
- pinch ground ginger
- 2 tbsp mirin
- 3 tsp sesame oil
- 1 block very firm tofu, cut into thick slices
- ½ tbsp rapeseed oil
- 2 courgettes, sliced horizontally into strips
- 200g Tenderstem broccoli
- black and white sesame seeds, to serve

1 Mix the soy sauce, soft brown sugar, ginger and mirin with 1 tsp sesame oil and brush it all over the slices of tofu. Put them in a large, shallow dish and pour over any leftover marinade. Chill for at least an hour.

2 Heat the barbecue until the coals are glowing white, or heat a griddle pan. Mix the remaining sesame oil with the rapeseed oil and brush the courgette slices and broccoli. Barbecue (or griddle) them over the coals for 7–10 mins or until they are tender and then set aside and keep warm.

3 Barbecue the tofu slices on both sides over the coals for 5 mins (or use the griddle) until they turn brown and go crisp at the edges. Serve the tofu on a bed of the veg with the remaining marinade and scatter over the black and white sesame seeds.

Nutrition per serving
Kcals 366 • fat 20g • saturates 1g • carbs 19g • sugars 16g • fibre 3g • protein 25g • salt 1.74g

Black bean chilli

This chilli is great for casual entertaining – just lay everything out and let people add their own toppings.

⏱ TAKES 40 mins ◔ SERVES 4–6

- 2 tbsp olive oil
- 4 garlic cloves, finely chopped
- 2 large onions, chopped
- 3 tbsp sweet paprika
- 3 tbsp ground cumin
- 3 tbsp cider vinegar
- 2 tbsp brown sugar
- 2 x 400g cans chopped tomatoes
- 2 x 400g cans black beans, rinsed and drained
- a few, or one, of the following to serve: cooked basmati rice, crumbled vegan cheese, chopped spring onions, sliced radishes, avocado chunks

1 In a large pot, heat the olive oil and fry the garlic and onions for 5 mins until almost softened. Add the paprika and cumin, cook for a few mins, then add the vinegar, sugar, tomatoes and some seasoning. Cook for 10 mins.
2 Pour in the beans and cook for another 10 mins. Serve with rice and the accompaniments of your choice in small bowls.

Nutrition per serving
Kcals 339 • fat 10g • saturates 1g • carbs 50g • sugars 20g • fibre 8g • protein 17g • salt 1.45g

Seitan & black bean stir-fry

This handy stir-fry makes a satisfying supper, with a sticky sweet and spicy sauce. Seitan, peanut butter and a mix of veggies is a winning combination.

 TAKES 45 mins SERVES 4

FOR THE SAUCE
- 400g can black beans, drained and rinsed
- 75g soft dark brown sugar
- 3 garlic cloves
- 2 tbsp soy sauce
- 1 tsp Chinese five-spice powder
- 2 tbsp rice vinegar
- 1 tbsp smooth peanut butter
- 1 red chilli, finely chopped

FOR THE STIR-FRY
- 350g jar marinated seitan pieces
- 1 tbsp cornflour
- 2–3 tbsp vegetable oil
- 2 shallots, chopped
- 1 red pepper, sliced
- 300g pak choi, chopped
- 2 spring onions, sliced
- cooked rice noodles or rice, to serve

1 Start by making the sauce: tip half the beans into the bowl of a food processor with the rest of the ingredients and add 50ml water. Season, then blend until smooth. Pour into a saucepan and heat gently for about 5 mins or until thick and glossy.

2 Drain the seitan and pat dry with kitchen paper. Toss the seitan pieces in a bowl with the cornflour and set aside. Heat your wok to a high temperature, add a little oil, then the seitan – you might need to do this in batches. Stir-fry for around 5 mins until golden brown at the edges. Remove the seitan from the wok using a slotted spoon and set aside on a plate.

3 If the wok is dry at this stage, add 1 tsp vegetable oil. Add the shallots and stir-fry until soft. Throw in the sliced pepper, the rest of the beans, the pak choi and spring onions. Cook for 3–4 mins, then return the seitan to the pan, stir in the sauce and bring to the boil for 1 min. Serve with cooked rice or noodles.

Nutrition per serving
Kcals 326 • fat 8g • saturates 1g • carbs 37g • sugars 23g • fibre 7g • protein 22g • salt 3.08g

Charred spring onions & teriyaki tofu

Rustle up this teriyaki tofu served with wholegrain rice in just 30 minutes. Easy and low in fat, this dish is perfect for busy weeknights.

TAKES 30 mins   SERVES 2

- 150g wholegrain rice
- 50ml soy sauce
- 2 tbsp mirin
- ½ tsp grated ginger
- 1 tsp honey
- 350g firm tofu
- 1 bunch spring onions, ends trimmed
- 2 tsp sunflower oil
- ½ tsp sesame seeds
- 1 red chilli, sliced (optional)

1 Cook the rice according to pack instructions. Pour the soy sauce, mirin, ginger and honey into a small saucepan and add 50ml water. Bring to a simmer and cook for around 5 mins or until slightly thickened. Remove from the heat and set aside until needed.

2 If your tofu doesn't feel very firm, you'll need to press it. To do this, wrap the block of tofu in a few layers of kitchen paper, then weigh it down with a heavy pan or tray for 10–15 mins – the longer you press it, the firmer it will be. Cut the tofu into thick slices.

3 Heat a griddle pan over a high heat and lightly brush the tofu and spring onions with the oil. Griddle the tofu and spring onion until deep char lines appear on both sides (around 4 mins each side) – you may have to do this in batches depending on the size of your griddle pan.

4 Divide the cooked rice between two plates, top with the tofu and spring onions, then drizzle with the teriyaki sauce. Garnish with the sesame seeds and sliced red chilli, if using.

Nutrition per serving
Kcals 507 • fat 11g • saturates 2g • carbs 76g • sugars 16g • fibre 5g • protein 23g • salt 3.5g

Roasted aubergine & tomato curry

Slightly sweet with added richness from the coconut milk, this simple vegan curry is a winner. It's also freezable if you need a quick midweek fix.

 TAKES 1 hr SERVES 4

- 600g baby aubergines, sliced into rounds
- 3 tbsp olive oil
- 2 onions, finely sliced
- 2 garlic cloves, crushed
- 1 tsp garam masala
- 1 tsp turmeric
- 1 tsp ground coriander
- 400g can chopped tomatoes
- 400g can coconut milk
- pinch of sugar (optional)
- ½ small pack coriander, roughly chopped
- rice or chapatis, to serve

1 Heat oven to 200C/180C fan/gas 6. Toss the aubergines in a roasting tin with 2 tbsp olive oil, season well and spread out. Roast for 20 mins or until dark golden and soft.

2 Heat the remaining oil in an ovenproof pan or flameproof casserole dish and cook the onions over a medium heat for 5–6 mins until softening. Stir in the garlic and spices and cook for a few mins until the spices release their aromas.

3 Tip in the tomatoes, coconut milk and roasted aubergines, and bring to a gentle simmer. Simmer for 20–25 mins, removing the lid for the final 5 mins to thicken the sauce. Add a little seasoning if you like, and a pinch of sugar if it needs it. Stir through most of the coriander. Serve over rice or with chapatis, scattering with the remaining coriander.

Nutrition per serving
Kcals 331 • fat 26g • saturates 16g • carbs 15g • sugars 12g • fibre 7g • protein 5g • salt 0g

Ginger aubergine miso noodles

Chunks of aubergine are pan-fried with Asian flavours, then stirred into soba noodles for a vegan supper.

TAKES 15 mins SERVES 4

- 400g soba noodles
- 1 tbsp sunflower oil
- 2 aubergines, diced
- 4cm piece ginger, grated
- 100g brown rice miso paste
- 2 tbsp sesame oil
- 2 tbsp mirin
- 1 tsp sugar
- 1 tbsp rice wine vinegar
- ½ bunch spring onions, sliced diagonally

1 Bring a pan of water to the boil and cook the noodles following pack instructions. Meanwhile, heat the sunflower oil in a frying pan. Cook the aubergines over a medium heat for 5–8 mins until softened.

2 Mix together the ginger, miso paste, sesame oil, mirin and sugar, add to the pan with the aubergines and cook for a few mins. Drain the cooked soba noodles and add to the pan, toss together, then divide between serving plates and scatter with the spring onions.

Nutrition per serving
Kcals 518 • fat 12g • saturates 2g • carbs 82g • sugars 11g • fibre 8g • protein 15g • salt 5.1g

Linguine with avocado, tomato & lime

Use guacamole ingredients to make this low-calorie vegan linguine, which can also be served cold as a pasta salad. It delivers on flavour and it's healthy.

🕐 TAKES 30 mins 🕐 SERVES 2

- 115g wholemeal linguine
- 1 lime, zested and juiced
- 1 avocado, stoned, peeled, and chopped
- 2 large ripe tomatoes, chopped
- ½ pack fresh coriander, chopped
- 1 red onion, finely chopped
- 1 red chilli, deseeded and finely chopped (optional)

1 Cook the pasta according to pack instructions – about 10 mins. Meanwhile, put the lime juice and zest in a medium bowl with the avocado, tomatoes, coriander, onion and chilli, if using, and mix well.

2 Drain the pasta, toss into the bowl and mix well. Serve straight away while still warm, or cold.

Nutrition per serving
Kcals 450 • fat 20g • saturates 4g • carbs 49g • sugars 11g • fibre 13g • protein 11g • salt 0.4g

Cauliflower steaks with roasted red pepper & olive salsa

Unlock the flavours of cauliflower with a red pepper, olive and caper salsa, topped with almonds. Healthy and vegan, it makes a tasty light lunch or supper.

🕐 TAKES 35 mins 🥧 SERVES 2

- 1 cauliflower
- ½ tsp smoked paprika
- 2 tbsp olive oil
- 1 roasted red pepper
- 4 black olives, pitted
- small handful parsley
- 1 tsp capers
- ½ tbsp red wine vinegar
- 2 tbsp toasted flaked almonds

1 Heat oven to 220C/200C fan/gas 7 and line a baking tray with baking parchment. Slice the cauliflower into two 1-inch steaks – use the middle part as it's larger, and save the rest for another time. Rub the paprika and ½ tbsp oil over the steaks and season. Put on the tray and roast for 15–20 mins until cooked through.

2 Meanwhile, make the salsa. Chop the pepper, olives, parsley and capers, and put into a bowl and mix with the remaining oil and vinegar. Season to taste. When the steaks are cooked, spoon over the salsa and top with flaked almonds to serve.

Nutrition per serving
Kcals 277 • fat 21g • saturates 2g • carbs 11g • sugars 6g • fibre 4g • protein 9g • salt 0.3g

Egyptian courgettes with dukkah sprinkle

Get all 5 of your 5-a-day in one vegan dinner! This easy recipe is healthy and gluten-free, and provides calcium, folate, fibre, vitamin C and iron.

🕐 TAKES 35 mins ⏱ SERVES 4

- 1 tbsp rapeseed oil
- 2 onions, halved and sliced
- 2 tsp ground coriander
- 2 tsp smoked paprika
- 400g can chopped tomatoes
- 2 tsp vegetable bouillon powder
- 2 large courgettes, sliced
- 400g can butter beans, drained
- 180g cherry tomatoes
- 160g frozen peas
- 15g coriander, chopped

FOR THE DUKKAH
- 1 tsp coriander seeds
- 1 tsp cumin seeds
- 1 tbsp sesame seeds
- 25g flaked almonds

1 Heat the oil in a large non-stick pan and fry the onions for 5 mins, stirring occasionally until starting to colour. Stir in the ground coriander and paprika, then tip in the tomatoes with a can of water. Add the bouillon powder and courgettes, cover and cook for 6 mins.

2 Meanwhile, make the dukkah. Warm the whole spices, sesame seeds and almonds in a pan until aromatic, stirring frequently, then remove the pan from the heat.

3 Add the butter beans, tomatoes and peas to the courgettes, cover and cook for 5 mins more. Stir in the coriander, then spoon into bowls. Crush the spices and almonds using a pestle and mortar and scatter on top. If you're cooking for 2 people, put half the seed mix in a jar and chill half the veg for another day.

Nutrition per serving
Kcals 521 • fat 20g • saturates 2g • carbs 47g • sugars 27g • fibre 23g • protein 26g • salt 0.3g

Vegan mac'n'cheese

Make the ultimate comfort dish, macaroni cheese, but with vegan credentials. The recipe is quick and easy to make, so is a great midweek meal for the family.

 TAKES 35 mins plus overnight soaking SERVES 6

- 160g raw cashews
- 200g carrots, peeled and cut into 1cm cubes
- 700g potatoes, peeled and cut into 1cm cubes
- 90ml olive oil
- 40g nutritional yeast
- 1 lemon, juice only
- 4 garlic cloves, peeled and roughly chopped
- 1 tbsp Dijon mustard
- 1 tbsp white wine vinegar
- 1 tsp cayenne pepper
- 400g macaroni
- 3 tbsp panko breadcrumbs

1 The night before, soak the cashew nuts in water and leave overnight.
2 Heat the oven to 180C/160C fan/gas 4. Steam the carrots and potatoes together for 5 mins, until completely softened Transfer to a food processor. Drain the cashews and add these with 60ml of the oil, then blitz to break down the nuts. Tip in the other ingredients – apart from the macaroni, breadcrumbs and the remaining oil – then blitz again until the mixture is smooth and season well. Add a splash of water and just a drizzle of olive oil if it looks too stiff, then set aside.
3 Cook the macaroni in a large pan of salted water for 1 min less than packet instructions, drain then stir through the sauce. Transfer the mix to an ovenproof dish, stir the breadcrumbs with the remaining oil and some seasoning. Scatter over the top of the macaroni and bake for 20–25 mins until piping hot and crisp.

Nutrition per serving
Kcals 686 • fat 30g • saturates 5g • carbs 80g • sugars 6g • fibre 8g • protein 20g • salt 1.12g

Tomato, runner bean & coconut curry

Pack 3 of your 5-a-day into this Indian-style one-pot with red lentils, coconut milk and zesty lime.

 TAKES 45 mins SERVES 4

- 1 tbsp vegetable or rapeseed oil
- 1 large onion, finely chopped
- 2 tbsp mild tandoori curry paste
- small pack coriander, stalks finely chopped, leaves roughly chopped
- 2 limes, 1 zested and juiced, 1 cut into wedges
- 200g red lentils
- 400ml can coconut milk
- 300g basmati rice
- 400g cherry tomatoes, halved
- 300g stringless runner beans, thinly sliced on the diagonal

1 Heat the oil in a large, heavy-based saucepan. Add the onion and cook for 5–10 mins on a medium heat until softened. Add the paste, coriander stalks and lime zest, and cook for 1–2 mins until fragrant. Tip in the red lentils, coconut milk and 400ml hot water, and bring to the boil. Turn down the heat and simmer for 15 mins. Meanwhile, put a pan of water on to boil and cook the rice following pack instructions.

2 Add the tomatoes and runner beans to the lentils and cook for a further 5 mins. Drain the rice. Add the lime juice to the curry, check the seasoning and sprinkle over the coriander leaves. Serve with the rice and lime wedges for squeezing over.

Nutrition per serving
Kcals 716 • fat 24g • saturates 16g • carbs 98g • sugars 10g • fibre 9g • protein 22g • salt 0.6g

CHAPTER 4: WEEKEND SUPPERS

At the weekend, you may have a little more time to create a special dinner for friends and family, and these recipes can help you do just that. Whether you want to ditch the takeaway and make your own curry, burger or pizza, or fancy trying a new ingredient like jackfruit, there's plenty of inspiration in this chapter. You'll also find dishes for Christmas celebrations.

Parsnip gnocchi

Take parsnips to another level by turning them into gnocchi with a crunchy walnut crumb. This dish is vegan, healthy and deliciously festive.

🕐 TAKES 1 hr 35 mins ◳ SERVES 4

- 400g parsnips, peeled and cut into chunks
- 600g potatoes, peeled and cut into chunks
- 60ml olive oil, plus a drizzle to serve
- 3 unpeeled garlic cloves
- 1 tsp ground nutmeg (around 1 clove)
- 100g '00' flour
- 2 tbsp nutritional yeast
- ½ small pack thyme, leaves picked, to serve
- 30g walnuts, toasted and chopped, to serve

1 Heat oven to 220C/200C fan/gas 7. Toss the parsnips and potatoes in 2 tbsp of the olive oil and tip into a roasting tin along with the garlic cloves. Roast for 40 mins or until the veg is completely soft. Remove from the oven and leave to cool a little. Squeeze the garlic from their skins, then discard the skins. Tip everything into a food processor, along with the ground nutmeg, flour and nutritional yeast, season well, then pulse until well combined and holding together as a dough.

2 Bring a large pan of salted water to the boil. Tip the dough onto a floured surface, cut into four chunks and roll each into a sausage about 35cm long and 2.5cm wide. Use the back of a table knife to cut each sausage into small pillow-shaped gnocchi, each around 2cm long. Cook the gnocchi in batches for 1 min or until they float to the surface. Remove from the water with a slotted spoon and drain on kitchen paper.

3 In a frying pan, heat the rest of the oil over a medium heat until shimmering. Add half the gnocchi and fry until lightly golden on each side, around 3–4 mins. Transfer them to a tray using a slotted spoon while you cook the second batch. When all the gnocchi are golden, return them all to the pan to warm through before dividing between four plates. Sprinkle over some black pepper, then top with the thyme leaves, toasted walnuts and a drizzle of olive oil, if you like.

Nutrition per serving
Kcals 525 • fat 22g • saturates 3g • carbs 63g • sugars 7g • fibre 11g • protein 12g • Salt 0.3g

Easy vegan burgers

Make vegan burgers with polenta and spice with cumin, chilli and coriander. Cook in the oven or on the barbecue and serve with a salsa.

🕐 TAKES 1 hr plus 30 mins chilling ◔ SERVES 10

- 6 large sweet potatoes (about 1½kg)
- 2 tsp oil, plus extra for the trays
- 2 red onions, finely chopped
- 2 red chillies, finely chopped (deseeded if you like)
- 1 tbsp ground cumin
- 1 tbsp ground coriander
- 340g can sweetcorn, drained
- small bunch coriander, chopped
- 200g polenta
- buns, salsa, onion and salad leaves, to serve

1 Heat oven to 200C/180C fan/gas 6. Pierce the potato skins and place on a baking tray. Bake for 45 mins until really soft. Remove from the oven and leave to cool. Meanwhile, heat the oil in a small pan, add the onions and chillies, and cook for 8–10 mins until soft. Leave to cool.

2 Peel the potatoes and add the flesh to a bowl with the chilli onions. Mash together with the spices until smooth. Using your hands, mix in the sweetcorn, coriander, half the polenta and some seasoning. Shape the mixture into 10 burgers; it will be quite soft. Carefully dip each one into the remaining polenta; dust off any excess. Place the burgers on oiled baking trays and chill for at least 30 mins. You can wrap and freeze the burgers at this stage.

3 Light the barbecue. When the flames have died down, place a large, well-oiled non-stick frying pan or sturdy baking tray on top of the bars. Cook the burgers in the pan or on the tray for 10 mins each side until nicely browned. Alternatively, heat oven to 220C/200C fan/gas 7 and cook on oiled baking trays for 15 mins. Serve in buns with a dollop of salsa, some onion and salad leaves.

Nutrition per burger
Kcals 252 • fat 2g • saturates 0g • carbs 54g • sugars 12g • fibre 6g • protein 5g • salt 0.4g

Squash steaks with chestnut & cavolo nero pilaf

If you're feeling like a lazy supper, this easy squash recipe is deliciously spiced. Serve with a dollop of coconut yoghurt.

 TAKES 1 hr 5 mins SERVES 4

- 1 butternut squash
- 2–3 tbsp olive oil, plus extra for frying
- ½ tsp smoked paprika, plus a little extra for sprinkling
- 200g cavolo nero or curly kale, shredded
- 1 onion, chopped
- 180g chestnuts, halved
- 2 garlic cloves, finely chopped
- ½ tsp ground cumin
- ½ tsp ground cinnamon
- 250g basmati rice and wild rice
- 500ml vegetable stock
- 150g pot coconut yoghurt

1 Heat oven to 220C/200C fan/gas 7. Cut the neck of the squash into 4 rounds (keep the rest for another time). Heat the oil in a large frying pan and brown the squash for a few mins each side. Transfer to a baking tray, sprinkle with half the paprika and roast for 30 mins.

2 Meanwhile, in the same frying pan, add a little extra oil and stir-fry the cavolo nero for 2 mins, then remove with a slotted spoon and set aside. Add the onion and chestnuts to the pan, cook for a few mins, then stir in the garlic, remaining paprika and spices and cook for 1 min. Stir in the rice and stock, bring to the boil, then cover with a lid. Turn the heat down as low as it will go and cook for 25 mins, stirring occasionally.

3 Once cooked, stir through the cavolo nero and serve with the squash steaks and the coconut yoghurt sprinkled with paprika.

Nutrition per serving
Kcals 562 • fat 15g • saturates 8g • carbs 87g • sugars 14g • fibre 10g • protein 14g • salt 0.4g

Roasted stuffed cauliflower

Need an alternative to nut roast for veggies and vegans? Try this filling cauliflower roast stuffed with kale and chestnuts.

⏱ TAKES 1 hr 30 mins ◔ SERVES 6

- 1 large or 2 small cauliflowers (about 850g)
- 5 tbsp olive oil
- 4 tbsp breadcrumbs

FOR THE STUFFING
- 250g kale, chopped
- 1 tbsp milled linseed
- 1 onion, chopped
- 2 garlic cloves, chopped
- ½ small pack sage, leaves chopped
- ½ small pack rosemary, leaves chopped
- 150g cooked chestnuts, finely chopped, plus 30g for the topping
- 2 lemons, zested
- good grating of nutmeg

1 Trim and discard the cauliflower leaves. Turn the cauliflower upside-down on a chopping board and use your knife to carefully cut out the stalk and core, leaving a cavity – the florets should still be holding together.

2 Bring a large pan of salted water to the boil. Submerge the cauliflower and cook for 7 mins, then remove with 2 slotted spoons and set aside to steam dry. Add the kale to the pan and cook for a min or so until wilted. Drain, then run under cold water to cool. Squeeze out the excess liquid and roughly chop.

3 To make a linseed 'egg' (this will bind the stuffing together), mix the ground linseed with 3 tbsp water and set aside for 5–10 mins until gluey. Meanwhile, heat 2 tbsp oil in a frying pan, add the onion and a pinch of salt, and cook until softened, then stir in the remaining stuffing ingredients, including the kale, and cook for a min or so more. Remove from the heat and season, then put in a blender with 150ml water and the linseed egg and blitz to a thick purée. Transfer to a piping bag.

4 Pipe the stuffing mixture into every nook and cranny of the cauliflower, getting in as much of the purée as you can. Transfer to a baking tray lined with parchment. Can be made up to this point in the morning and kept in the fridge.

5 Heat oven to 200C/180C fan/gas 6. Mix the remaining chestnuts with the breadcrumbs and some seasoning. Spoon the remaining oil all over the cauliflower, then pat on the breadcrumb chestnut mix. Roast for 45 mins until golden brown and tender (place under a hot grill for the last part of cooking time if it needs to crisp-up). Serve with any crisp bits that have fallen onto the baking tray.

Nutrition per serving
Kcals 261 • fat 12g • saturates 2g • carbs 27g • sugars 8g • fibre 7g • protein 6g • salt 0.4g

Beetroot & squash Wellingtons with kale pesto

Put some welly in your dinner. Make these vegan Wellingtons ahead of time for a less stressed Sunday feast. Even the meat eaters will love them!

TAKES 2 hrs plus 1 hr or overnight chilling SERVES 6

- 1 red onion, cut into 8 wedges
- 250g raw beetroot, peeled and cut into small chunks
- ½ butternut squash, peeled and cut into small chunks
- 4 fat garlic cloves, unpeeled
- 6 tbsp olive oil
- 1 tbsp picked thyme leaves, plus extra for sprinkling
- 1 tbsp sumac, plus extra for sprinkling
- 250g pouch ready-to-eat Puy lentils
- 180g pack whole cooked chestnuts, roughly chopped
- 100g kale
- ½ lemon, juiced
- 2 x 320g packs ready-rolled puff pastry suitable for vegans
- 2 tbsp almond milk

1 Heat oven to 190C/170C fan/gas 5. Toss the onion, beetroot, squash and garlic in a roasting tin with 2 tbsp of the olive oil, the thyme leaves, sumac and some seasoning. Roast for 45 mins until the vegetables are tender but still retain their shape, then stir in the lentils and half the chestnuts.

2 Squeeze the garlic cloves from their skins, reserve half and squash the other 2 into the lentil mixture. Leave the lentils to cool completely.

3 Bring a large pan of salted water to the boil, tip in the kale, cook for 1 min until wilted, then drain and run under cold water until cool. Squeeze all the water from the kale, then put it in the small bowl of a food processor along with the reserved garlic cloves, chestnuts, the lemon juice, olive oil and some seasoning. Blitz to a thick pesto and season to taste.

4 On a lightly floured surface, unravel the sheets of puff pastry. Cut each sheet into 3 widthways so that you have 6 strips in total then divide the kale pesto among these, followed by the roasted veg and lentils, heaping the mixture on top of the pesto and leaving one side free of filling so that it is easier to roll. Brush all the borders with half the milk, fold over the ends, then carefully roll the pastry lengthways to completely encase the filling into a roll. Place your 6 individual Wellingtons on a baking tray lined with baking parchment and chill for at least 1 hr, or cover with cling film and leave overnight. If freezing, cover and freeze on a lined baking tray for up to 3 months.

5 To bake from chilled, heat oven to 190 C/170 C fan/gas 5 and line a baking tray with baking parchment.

6 Brush the top of each Wellington with the remaining milk and sprinkle with a little sumac, then bake for 30 mins from chilled or 45 mins from frozen until crisp and golden. Scatter over extra thyme and some flaky sea salt and serve.

Nutrition per serving
Kcals 669 • fat 38g • saturates 15g • carbs 63g • sugars 8g • fibre 8g • protein 13g • salt 1.5g

White pizza

Make this pizza using tofu, almond milk and other clever, dairy-free options. Choose from a range of toppings and sprinkle with fresh or dried herbs.

TAKES 30 mins plus 1 hr rising MAKES 2 large or 4 small pizzas (SERVES 4)

FOR THE PIZZA DOUGH
- 500g strong white bread flour, plus extra for dusting
- 1 tsp dried yeast
- 1 tsp caster sugar
- 1½ tbsp olive oil, plus extra

FOR THE WHITE SAUCE
- 150g silken tofu
- 100ml almond milk
- 1 garlic clove, crushed
- ¼ tsp nutmeg
- 1–2 tsp lemon juice

OPTIONAL TOPPINGS
- 1 sliced courgette, red chilli flakes, 2 tbsp nutritional yeast, rosemary sprigs, grated vegan pizza cheese, handful fresh spinach leaves, cooked and cooled new potatoes, sliced

TO SERVE
- fresh basil or oregano leaves, chilli oil and vegan parmesan

1 Put the flour, yeast and sugar in a large bowl. Measure 150ml of cold water and 150ml boiling water into a jug and mix them together – this will mean your water is a good temperature for the yeast. Add the oil and 1 tsp salt to the warm water then pour it over the flour. Stir well with a spoon then start to knead the mixture together in the bowl until it forms a soft and slightly sticky dough. If it's too dry add a splash of cold water.

2 Dust a little flour on the work surface and knead the dough for 10 mins. Put it back in the mixing bowl and cover with cling film greased with a few drops of olive oil. Leave to rise in a warm place for 1 hr or until doubled in size.

3 Heat oven to 240C/220C/gas 9 and put a baking sheet or pizza stone on the top shelf to heat up. Once the dough has risen, knock it back by punching it a couple of times with your fist then kneading it again on a floured surface. It should be springy and a lot less sticky. Set aside while you prepare the white sauce.

4 Put all the ingredients for the sauce together in a blender (or in a jug and blend with a stick blender) and blend until smooth and slightly thickened.

5 Divide the dough into 2 or 4 pieces (depending on whether you want to make large or small pizzas), shape into balls and flatten each piece out as thin as you can get it with a rolling pin or using your hands. Make sure the dough is well dusted with flour to stop it sticking. Dust another baking sheet with flour then put a pizza base on top. Spread 5–6 tbsp of the white sauce mixture on top and add your chosen toppings, then drizzle with a little olive oil. Put it in the oven on top of your preheated baking tray and cook for 10–12 mins or until the base is puffed up and the sauce is starting to turn golden in patches.

6 Repeat with the rest of the dough and toppings – you may have a little white sauce left over, which will keep for the next day in the fridge. Serve the pizzas with fresh basil leaves or chilli oil if you like and sprinkle vegan parmesan over the top just after baking.

(Nutrition per serving (excluding toppings)
Kcals 543 • fat 8g • saturates 1g • carbs 97g • sugars 2g • fibre 4g • protein 18g • salt 1.3g

Vegan shepherd's pie

A warming supper with porcini mushrooms, leeks, carrots, butternut squash and plenty of herbs, topped with crispy potatoes – it's low-calorie, low-fat and perfect for when the nights draw in.

🕐 TAKES 1 hr 50 mins ⎙ SERVES 8

- 1.2kg floury potatoes, such as Maris Piper or King Edward
- 50ml vegetable oil
- 30g dried porcini mushrooms, soaked in hot water for 15 mins, then drained (reserve the liquid)
- 2 large leeks, chopped
- 2 small onions, chopped
- 4 medium carrots (about 300g), cut into small cubes
- 1 vegan stock cube
- 3 garlic cloves, crushed
- 2 tbsp tomato purée
- 2 tsp smoked paprika
- 1 small butternut squash, peeled and cut into small cubes
- ½ small pack marjoram or oregano, leaves picked and roughly chopped
- ½ small pack thyme, leaves picked
- ½ small pack sage, leaves roughly chopped
- 4 celery sticks, chopped
- 400g can chickpeas
- 300g frozen peas
- 300g frozen spinach
- 20ml olive oil
- small pack flat-leaf parsley, chopped
- tomato ketchup, to serve (optional)

1 Put the unpeeled potatoes in a large saucepan, cover with water, bring to the boil and simmer for 40 mins until the skin start to split. Drain and leave to cool a little. Heat oven to 190C/170C fan/gas 5.

2 Meanwhile, heat the vegetable oil in a large heavy-based sauté pan or flameproof casserole dish. Add the mushrooms, leeks, onions, carrots and the stock cube and cook gently for 5 mins, stirring every so often. If it starts to stick, reduce the heat and stir more frequently, scraping the bits from the bottom. The vegetables should be soft but not mushy.

3 Add the garlic, tomato purée, paprika, squash and herbs. Stir and turn the heat up a bit, cook for 3 mins, add the celery, then stir and cook for a few more mins.

4 Tip in the chickpeas along with the water in the can and reserved mushroom stock. Add the peas and spinach and stir well. Cook for 5 mins, stirring occasionally, then season, turn off the heat and set aside. There should still be plenty of liquid and the veg should be bright and a little firm.

5 Peel the potatoes and discard the skin. Mash 200g with a fork and stir into the veg. Break the rest of the potatoes into chunks, mix with the olive oil and parsley and season.

6 Tip the filling into a pie dish and top with the potatoes. Bake for 40–45 mins, until the top is golden and the filling is heated through. If making individual pies, check after 20 mins. Best served with tomato ketchup – as all great shepherd's pies are.

Nutrition per serving
Kcals 348 • fat 11g • saturates 1g • carbs 43g • sugars 10g • fibre 13g • protein 11g • salt 0.5g

'Cheesy' leek crumble

Cook a vegan bake with bags of cheese and onion flavour. Nutritional yeast gives you the tangy umami hit that will keep dairy lovers guessing.

TAKES 1 hr 15 mins plus overnight soaking   SERVES 6

- 80g unsalted cashews
- 100g carrots, cut into 1cm cubes
- 350g potatoes, cut into 1cm cubes
- 60ml olive oil
- 5 tbsp nutritional yeast
- ½ lemon, juiced
- 2 garlic cloves
- 1 tsp English mustard
- 1 tsp vegan white wine vinegar
- 4 leeks (about 500g), sliced

FOR THE CRUMBLE
- 50g rolled oats
- 50g flour
- 25g unscented coconut oil, melted
- 3 tbsp chopped thyme leaves

1 The night before, soak the cashew nuts in water and leave overnight.
2 To make the crumble, tip the oats and flour into a bowl, make a well in the centre and pour in the coconut oil. Draw the dry ingredients in until everything is well coated and resembles chunky breadcrumbs. Tip the mixture onto a baking sheet and put in the fridge to firm up – this will make your topping extra crunchy.
3 Heat oven to 200C/180C fan/gas 6. Steam the carrots and potatoes together for 5 mins until softened, then transfer to a food processor. Drain the cashews and add them too, along with 2 tbsp oil and the rest of the sauce ingredients except for the leeks. Blitz the mixture, season and set aside.
4 Heat the remaining oil in a large frying pan over a medium heat. Add the leeks and a large pinch of salt, then fry for 15 mins until softened. Spoon in the cheese sauce – if it is very thick, add a splash of water to thin it. Transfer the mix to an ovenproof dish, top with the crumble and bake for 30 mins until piping hot. For a crispy topping, put under the grill to finish. Can be assembled in advance and kept in the fridge to cook when needed.

Nutrition per serving
Kcals 400 • fat 23g • saturates 7g • carbs 31g • sugars 4g • fibre 8g • protein 13g • salt 0.5g

Thai noodle curry

An easy vegan version of a Thai noodle curry, packed with vegetables, coconut milk, chilli and spices to make a flavoursome, warming family meal.

🕐 TAKES 40 mins ◔ SERVES 3

FOR THE PASTE

- 2 lemongrass stalks, tough outer leaves removed, core finely chopped
- 5 spring onions, chopped
- handful fresh coriander, chopped
- 8 dried kaffir lime leaves
- 2 tbsp tamari
- 2 green chillies, deseeded
- thumb-sized piece ginger, chopped

FOR THE CURRY

- 2 aubergines, roughly chopped
- 1 red pepper, roughly chopped
- 2 tbsp coconut oil, melted
- 1 tbsp sesame oil
- 250g green beans, cut into thirds
- 300ml vegetable stock
- 400ml can unhomogenised coconut milk (cream only)
- 300g buckwheat noodles
- handful cashew nuts
- 4 tbsp desiccated coconut
- 1 lime and finely chopped red chilli, to serve

1. Heat oven to 200C/180C fan/gas 6. To make the curry, toss the aubergines and red pepper in a roasting tin with 1 tbsp coconut oil and roast for 20–25 mins until softened.
2. Meanwhile, make the paste. Put all the ingredients in a food processor and blend until smooth.
3. Heat the sesame oil and remaining coconut oil in a frying pan or wok. Add the paste and fry for 1–2 mins, then stir in the green beans and fry for another 1–2 mins.
4. Add the vegetable stock, mixing well, followed by the roasted vegetables and the solid coconut cream from the top of the can of coconut milk. Give it all a good stir, bring to the boil, then allow it to simmer for 4–5 mins.
5. Meanwhile, cook the buckwheat noodles following the pack instructions.
6. Add the cashews and desiccated coconut to the curry. Divide the drained noodles among 3 bowls, top with the curry, squeeze over some lime juice and garnish with the red chilli.

Nutrition per serving
Kcals 951 • fat 49g • saturates 35g • carbs 91g • sugars 21g • fibre 21g • protein 25g • salt 3g

Kentucky fried seitan

Use a tofu substitute to make this addictive crispy fried 'chicken'. Try this delicious vegan party food with BBQ sauce, or in a bun with salad or coleslaw.

TAKES 1 hr 45 mins   SERVES 4-6

- 250g firm tofu
- 150ml unsweetened soya milk
- 2 tsp miso paste
- 2 tsp Marmite
- 1 tsp dried tarragon
- 1 tsp dried sage
- 1 tsp dried thyme
- 1 tsp onion powder
- 2 tsp garlic powder
- 160g wheat gluten
- 40g pea protein or vegan protein powder
- 1½ litres vegetable stock
- 1 onion, quartered
- 3 garlic cloves
- handful parsley stalks
- 300g gram flour
- 350g plain flour
- vegetable or sunflower oil for frying

FOR THE SPICE COATING
- 2 tsp dried thyme
- 2 tsp dried basil
- 2 tsp dried oregano
- 2 tsp ground ginger
- 3 tsp celery salt
- 3 tsp black pepper
- 3 tsp white pepper
- 3 tsp dried mustard
- 3 tsp paprika
- 3 tsp dried sage
- 4 tsp garlic powder
- 1 tsp brown sugar
- 200g panko breadcrumbs

1 First, make the seitan. Blitz the tofu, soya milk, miso, Marmite, tarragon, sage, thyme, onion powder, garlic powder, 1 tsp salt and ½ tsp white pepper in a food processor until smooth.

2 Tip into a bowl and add the wheat gluten and pea protein or protein powder. Mix to form a dough. Once it has come together, give it a really good knead, stretching and tearing for 10–15 mins. It will be ready when the seitan feels springy.

3 Pour the veg stock into a pan with the onion, garlic and parsley stalks. Bring to a simmer. Flatten out the seitan to 1cm in thickness, and chop into chicken-breast-sized chunks. Simmer these in the stock for 30 mins, covered with a lid. Allow to cool in the stock. Ideally do this the day before and chill in the fridge. These can also be frozen if you wish.

4 Mix the spice coating ingredients in one bowl. Place the gram flour in another and the plain flour in a third. Mix enough water into the gram flour until it has a texture similar to beaten egg. Dip the seitan pieces in the plain flour, shake off the excess, then coat each piece in the gram flour mixture and finally in the panko spice coating.

5 In a large frying pan or deep fat fryer, heat the oil to 180C (or until a piece of bread browns in 20 seconds). Once it's hot, carefully drop in the seitan pieces and cook for 6 mins or so until they are dark golden brown and crispy. Transfer to kitchen paper to drain off the excess oil and sprinkle with a little salt. Serve in toasted buns with salad or slaw, or alternatively as mock chicken dippers with BBQ sauce.

Nutrition per serving (6)
Kcals 777 · fat 15g · saturates 1g · carbs 97g · sugars 3g · fibre 10g · protein 59g · salt 3.62g

Pizza Margherita

Vegans needn't miss out on pizza Margherita. Our recipe combines the classic flavours of this Italian comfort food using plant-based substitutes.

TAKES 30 mins plus 1 hr rising MAKES 2 large or 4 small pizzas (SERVES 4)

FOR THE PIZZA DOUGH
- 500g strong white bread flour, plus extra for dusting
- 1 tsp dried yeast
- 1 tsp caster sugar
- 1½ tbsp olive oil, plus extra

FOR THE TOMATO SAUCE
- 100ml passata
- 1 tbsp fresh basil, chopped (or ½ tsp dried oregano)
- 1 garlic clove, crushed

FOR THE TOPPING
- 200g vegan mozzarella-style cheese, grated
- 2 tomatoes, thinly sliced
- Fresh basil or oregano leaves, chilli oil and vegan parmesan, to serve (optional)

1 Put the flour, yeast and sugar in a large bowl. Measure 150ml of cold water and 150ml boiling water into a jug and mix them together – this will mean your water is a good temperature for the yeast. Add the oil and 1 tsp salt to the warm water then pour it over the flour. Stir well with a spoon then start to knead the mixture together in the bowl until it forms a soft and slightly sticky dough. If it's too dry add a splash of cold water.

2 Dust a little flour on the work surface and knead the dough for 10 mins. Put it back in the mixing bowl and cover with cling film greased with a few drops of olive oil. Leave to rise in a warm place for 1 hr or until doubled in size.

3 Heat oven to 240C/220C fan/gas 9 and put a baking sheet or pizza stone on the top shelf to heat up. Once the dough has risen, knock it back by punching it a couple of times with your fist then kneading it again on a floured surface. It should be springy and a lot less sticky. Set aside while you prepare the sauce.

4 Put all the ingredients for the tomato sauce together in a bowl, season with salt, pepper and a pinch of sugar if you like and mix well. Set aside until needed.

5 Divide the dough into 2 or 4 pieces (depending on whether you want to make large or small pizzas), shape into balls and flatten each piece out as thin as you can get it with a rolling pin or using your hands. Make sure the dough is well dusted with flour to stop it sticking. Dust another baking sheet with flour then put a pizza base on top. Spread 4–5 tbsp of the tomato sauce on top and add some sliced tomatoes and grated vegan cheese. Drizzle with a little olive oil and bake in the oven on top of your preheated baking tray for 10–12 mins or until the base is puffed up and the vegan cheese has melted and is bubbling and golden in patches.

6 Repeat with the rest of the dough and topping. Serve the pizzas with fresh basil leaves or chilli oil if you like and sprinkle over vegan parmesan just after baking.

Nutrition per serving
Kcals 688 • fat 20g • saturates 11g • carbs 107g • sugars 4g • fibre 5g • protein 18g • salt 2g

Pulled jackfruit

Use jackfruit to make this clever vegan 'pulled' meat substitute, perfect for stuffing into bread rolls or tacos and enjoying with all the barbecue trimmings.

TAKES 1 hr · SERVES 4-6

- 1 tbsp vegetable oil
- 1 red onion, finely chopped
- 1 tsp ground cinnamon
- 1 tsp cumin seeds
- 2 tsp smoked paprika
- 2 tsp chipotle Tabasco
- 1 tbsp apple cider vinegar
- 4 tbsp BBQ sauce
- 200g can chopped tomatoes
- 2 x 400g cans young jackfruit in salted water, drained

1 Heat the oil in a frying pan and cook the onion until very soft, around 10–12 mins. Add the cinnamon, cumin and paprika to the onions and cook for a further 2–3 mins. Next add the Tabasco, vinegar and BBQ sauce and mix well before adding in the tomatoes, the drained jackfruit and 200ml water. Leave to simmer gently, covered, for 30 mins stirring every 5–10 mins to help break down the jackfruit, then take the lid off and cook a further 10 minutes.

2 Once cooked, use a fork to make sure all of the jackfruit is well shredded. Check seasoning and add another tbsp of BBQ sauce if necessary for extra stickiness.

Nutrition per serving
Kcals 135 · fat 2g · saturates 0g · carbs 26g · sugars 24g · fibre 2g · protein 1g · salt 0.3g

Nut roast

Combine root vegetables with mushrooms, grains, hazelnuts and fresh herbs to make this stunning vegan centrepiece. Top with parsnip crisps for added crunch.

🕐 TAKES 2 hrs 5 mins 📐 SERVES 6–8

- 150g pearl barley
- 1 vegan vegetable stock cube (check the packet)
- 330g parsnips, peeled and cut into chunks
- 2 tbsp ground linseeds (or flaxseed)
- 3 tbsp olive oil, plus extra for greasing
- 1 onion, halved and sliced
- 3 garlic cloves, crushed
- 400g mixed mushrooms, cleaned and sliced
- 1 rosemary sprig, leaves stripped, plus extra to decorate if you like
- 3 sage leaves, shredded
- 50g vegan Italian-style hard cheese, grated (optional)
- small pack flat-leaf parsley, finely chopped
- 100g blanched hazelnuts, toasted until golden
- good grating of nutmeg
- handful parsnip crisps with sea salt and black pepper (optional)
- 3 tbsp pumpkin seeds

1 Cook the pearl barley with the stock cube according to pack instructions. Reserve 4 tbsp of the cooking stock, then drain the grains well.

2 Bring a large pan of salted water to the boil, then add the parsnips and cook until really soft. Drain well, tip back into the pan to steam dry for a few minutes, then roughly mash. Mix the ground linseeds with the reserved stock water, and leave to go gluey.

3 Put 2 tbsp of the oil in your largest frying pan with the onions and garlic. Fry gently until soft and golden, then stir in the mushrooms, rosemary and sage and fry until the mushrooms are golden too, and any liquid that comes out has evaporated. Scrape into a big mixing bowl and set aside to cool.

4 Grease a 22–24cm savarin or ring tin generously with oil. If it's not a non-stick tin, line it with thin strips of overlapping baking parchment.

5 Add the mashed parsnip, cooked pearl barley, gluey seed mix, grated vegan hard cheese (if using), chopped parsley and whole hazelnuts to the fried mushroom mixture. Season generously with salt and nutmeg, then mix everything together really well.

6 Spoon the filling into the tin, and press down firmly to fill the tin and flatten the top. Keep in the fridge for up to 24 hrs before baking.

7 Heat the oven to 200C/180C fan/gas 6 and cover the tin with foil. Bake for 45 mins until a skewer poked into the centre of the mixture comes out piping hot.

8 Use a small palette knife or cutlery knife to release the filling all the way around, then sit a serving plate on top and flip over. Carefully lift off the tin, and top the wreath with some parsnip crisps (if using) and whole pumpkin seeds to serve – plus some extra rosemary sprigs if you like. Slice into wedges and enjoy.

Nutrition per serving (8)
Kcals 314 • fat 19g • saturates 3g • carbs 25g • sugars 4g • fibre 5g • protein 9g • salt 0.5g

Vegetable biriyani with carrot salad

A meat- and dairy-free, Indian-inspired basmati rice dish with cauliflower, green beans, peas, potatoes, homemade curry paste and carrot salad.

TAKES 40 mins plus 30 mins soaking SERVES 8

- 400g basmati rice
- pinch saffron threads (optional)
- 2 tbsp vegetable oil
- 1 cauliflower, cut into florets
- 2 potatoes, cut into chunks
- 100g red lentils
- 100g green beans, halved
- handful curry leaves
- 2 handfuls frozen peas
- small bunch coriander
- 50g roasted cashew nuts, roughly chopped
- poppadums and naan bread, to serve

FOR THE PASTE
- 1 large onion, roughly chopped
- large piece ginger, roughly chopped
- 5 garlic cloves
- 2 tsp curry powder
- 1 tsp ground cumin
- 2 tbsp vegetable oil
- 1 small green chilli

FOR THE CARROT SALAD
- 4 carrots
- pinch of golden caster sugar
- squeeze lemon juice
- handful cashew nuts, roughly chopped
- handful coriander leaves, roughly chopped
- thumb-sized piece ginger, shredded into matchsticks
- 1 tsp cumin seeds, toasted

1 Soak the rice for 30 mins, then rinse in several changes of water until it runs clear. Cover with about 1cm water, add the saffron (if using), cover the pan, bring to the boil, stir once, then turn off the heat. Leave for 10 mins, covered, then stir again and leave to stand, covered.

2 To make the paste, blitz all the ingredients together in a food processor.

3 Heat the oil in a saucepan. Tip in the paste, then add the cauliflower and potatoes. Cook in the paste to colour, then add the lentils and green beans and cover with about 400ml water. Add the curry leaves, season with salt, cover with a lid and simmer for 20 mins until the lentils and vegetables are tender Add the peas for the last 2 mins to defrost. Stir the rice through the curry until completely mixed and hot, then spoon onto a platter and scatter with coriander and cashews.

4 For the carrot salad, use a peeler to shave the carrots into ribbons. Sprinkle with the sugar and dress with the lemon juice, then toss with the other ingredients. Serve the biryani on a large platter for everyone to help themselves, with the carrot salad on the side, poppadoms for any vegans and naan bread for the vegetarians.

Nutrition per serving
Kcals 424 • fat 13g • saturates 2g • carbs 60g • sugars 9g • fibre 7g • protein 14g • salt 0.2g

Beetroot & red onion tarte tatin

Bake this vegan tart for a showstopper at a dinner party. The bold red of beetroot against the green salad also makes it ideal for a meat-free Christmas Day.

🕐 TAKES 1 hr 30 mins ◔ SERVES 4-6

- 400g beetroot, cut into wedges
- 1 red onion, cut into wedges
- 3 tbsp olive oil
- 2 tbsp rice wine vinegar
- 2 tbsp soft brown sugar
- 2 star anise
- flour, for rolling
- 500g block puff pastry suitable for vegans
- 1 orange, zested
- peppery green salad, to serve

1 Heat oven to 200C/180C fan/gas 6. In a bowl, toss the beetroot and onion in 2 tbsp of the oil, the vinegar and sugar. Add the star anise and season well. Heat the rest of the oil in a large, ovenproof non-stick frying pan, then nestle in the veg so that they cover the surface of the pan. Cover with foil and cook in the oven for 45 mins.

2 On a well-floured surface, roll the pastry to a thickness of 0.5cm and cut out a circle the same size as your frying pan Carefully take the pan out of the oven, remove the foil and wiggle the beets and onion around in the pan to make a compact layer. Put the pastry on top, tucking it in all around the edges, then return the pan to the oven and bake for 35 mins or until the pastry has puffed up and is a deep golden brown.

3 Slide a palette knife around the edge of the tart, then put a plate on top of the pastry, serving side down. Flip the pan over to turn the tart out onto the plate – be careful not to burn yourself with the handle. Top with the orange zest and a sprinkle of sea salt, then serve with a peppery salad on the side.

Nutrition per serving
Kcals 444 • fat 27g • saturates 11g • carbs 40g • sugars 14g • fibre 5g • protein 6g • salt 0.9g

Mushroom & chestnut rotolo

Serve this vegan bake for a dinner party. The honeycomb effect of rolled lasagne sheets looks fab and the crispy sage is delicious.

 TAKES 1 hr SERVES 4

- 30g dried mushrooms
- 240g chestnuts
- 6 tbsp olive oil
- 3 banana shallots, finely sliced
- 3 fat garlic cloves, crushed
- 3 rosemary sprigs
- 500g fresh wild mushrooms, brushed clean and roughly chopped
- 2 tbsp soy sauce
- 125ml vegan white wine
- 350g vegan dried lasagne sheets
- 4 tbsp panko breadcrumbs
- ½ small pack sage, leaves picked
- truffle oil (optional), to serve

1 Soak the dried mushrooms in 350ml boiling water and set aside until needed. Blitz ¾ of the chestnuts with 150ml water until creamy. Roughly chop the remaining chestnuts.

2 Heat 2 tbsp olive oil in a large non-stick frying pan. Fry the shallots with a pinch of salt until softened, then add the garlic, chopped chestnuts and rosemary, and fry for 2 mins more. Add the wild mushrooms, 2 tbsp oil and some seasoning. Cook for 3 mins until they begin to soften. Drain and roughly chop the dried mushrooms (reserve the soaking liquid), then add those too, along with the soy sauce, and fry for 2 mins more.

3 Whisk the wine, reserved mushroom liquid and chestnut cream together to create a sauce. Season, then add half to the mushroom mixture in the pan and cook for 1 min until the sauce becomes glossy. Remove and discard the rosemary sprigs, then set the mixture aside.

4 Heat oven to 180C/160C fan/gas 4. Bring a large pan of salted water to the boil and get a large bowl of ice water ready. Drop the lasagne sheets into the boiling water for 2 mins or until pliable and a little cooked, then immediately plunge them into the cold water. Using your fingers, carefully separate the sheets and transfer to a clean tea towel. Spread a good spoonful of the sauce on the bottom two thirds of each sheet, then, rolling away from yourself, roll up the shorter ends. Cut each roll in half, then position the rolls of pasta cut-side up in a pie dish that you are happy to serve from at the table. If you have any mushroom sauce remaining after you've rolled up all the sheets, simply push it into some of the exposed rolls of pasta.

5 Pour the rest of the sauce over the top of the pasta, then bake for 10 mins or until the pasta no longer has any resistance when tested with a skewer.

6 Meanwhile, put the breadcrumbs, the last 2 tbsp olive oil, sage leaves and some seasoning in a bowl, and toss everything together. Scatter the rotolo with the crumbs and sage, then bake for another 10 mins, until the top is golden and the sage leaves are crispy. Leave to cool for 10 mins to allow the pasta to absorb the sauce, then drizzle with a little truffle oil, if you like, before taking your dish to the table.

Nutrition per serving
Kcals 416 • fat 24g • saturates 3g • carbs 34g • sugars 10g • fibre 10g • protein 10g • salt 0.3g

Jerk sweet potato & black bean curry

Serve your vegetable curry Caribbean-style, flavoured with thyme, jerk seasoning and red peppers – great with rice and peas.

TAKES 50 mins SERVES 10

- 2 onions, 1 diced, 1 roughly chopped
- 2 tbsp sunflower oil
- 50g ginger, roughly chopped
- small bunch coriander, leaves and stalks separated
- 3 tbsp jerk seasoning
- 2 thyme sprigs
- 400g can chopped tomatoes
- 4 tbsp red wine vinegar
- 3 tbsp demerara sugar
- 2 vegan stock cubes, crumbled
- 1kg sweet potato, peeled and cut into chunks
- 2 x 400g cans black beans, rinsed and drained
- 450g jar roasted red peppers, cut into thick slices

1 Gently soften the diced onion in the sunflower oil in a big pan or casserole.

2 Meanwhile, whizz together the roughly chopped onion, ginger, coriander stalks and jerk seasoning with a hand blender. Add to the softened onion and fry until fragrant. Stir in the thyme, chopped tomatoes, vinegar, sugar and stock cubes with 600ml water and bring to a simmer. Simmer for 10 mins, then drop in the sweet potatoes and simmer for 10 mins more. Stir in the beans, peppers and some seasoning and simmer for another 5 mins until the potatoes are almost tender. Cool and chill for up to 2 days.

3 To serve, gently heat through on the hob. Roughly chop most of the coriander leaves and stir in, then serve scattered with the remaining leaves.

Nutrition per serving
Kcals 209 • fat 3g • saturates 1g • carbs 39g • sugars 14g • fibre 7g • protein 6g • salt 0.7g

Stuffed pumpkin

Throwing a vegan dinner party in the autumn or winter months? Bake a pumpkin with a gorgeous stuffing of rice, fennel, apple, pomegranate seeds and pecans.

TAKES 1 hr 15 mins SERVES 4

- 1 medium-sized pumpkin or round squash (about 1kg)
- 4 tbsp olive oil
- 100g wild rice
- 1 large fennel bulb
- 1 Bramley apple
- 1 lemon, zested and juiced
- 1 tbsp fennel seeds
- ½ tsp chilli flakes
- 2 garlic cloves, crushed
- 30g pecans, toasted and roughly chopped
- 1 large pack parsley, roughly chopped
- 3 tbsp tahini
- pomegranate seeds, to serve

1 Heat oven to 200C/180C fan/gas 6. Cut the top off the pumpkin or squash and use a metal spoon to scoop out the seeds. Get rid of any pithy bits but keep the seeds for another time. Put the pumpkin on a baking tray, rub with 2 tbsp of the oil inside and out, and season well. Roast in the centre of the oven for 45 mins or until tender, with the 'lid' on the side.

2 Meanwhile, rinse the wild rice well and cook following pack instructions, then spread out on a baking tray to cool. Thinly slice the fennel bulb and apple, then squeeze over ½ the lemon juice to stop them discolouring.

3 Heat the remaining 2 tbsp oil in a frying pan. Fry the fennel seeds and chilli flakes, then, once the seeds begin to pop, stir in ½ the garlic and the fennel. Cook for 5 mins until softened, then mix through the apple, pecans and lemon zest. Remove from the heat. Add the mixture to the cooked rice, then stir in the parsley and taste for seasoning.

4 Pack the mixture into the cooked pumpkin and return to the oven for 10–15 mins until everything is piping hot. Meanwhile, whisk the remaining lemon juice with the tahini, the rest of the garlic and enough water to make a dressing. Serve the pumpkin in the middle of the table, topped with pomegranate seeds and the dressing.

Nutrition per serving
Kcals 693 • fat 21g • saturates 3g • carbs 97g • sugars 10g • fibre 9g • protein 20g • salt 1.3g

Christmas wreath

· ·

Bake our vegan Christmas wreath with spinach, pine nuts and tofu as a centrepiece for a meat-free Christmas Day. Adorn with festive cranberries and dill.

🕐 TAKES 1 hr 10 mins 🕐 SERVES 6-8

- 250g spinach
- 250g silken tofu
- 2 tbsp extra virgin olive oil, plus extra for brushing
- 50g pine nuts, toasted
- generous grating nutmeg
- 2 fat garlic cloves, crushed
- 2 lemons, zested
- 1 small pack dill, ¾ leaves chopped, ¼ fronds reserved for decorating
- 1 tbsp sour cherries
- ½ tbsp dried cranberries, plus a few extra
- flour, for rolling
- 500g block shortcrust pastry suitable for vegans
- almond milk, for brushing

1 Put the spinach in a colander, then pour over a kettle of boiling water and leave to wilt. Once cool, wring out the excess moisture using a clean tea towel, then chop the spinach and put in a large bowl. Stir in the tofu, oil, pine nuts, nutmeg, garlic, lemon zest, chopped dill and fruit until well combined, season generously and set aside.

2 On a well-floured surface, roll the pastry out into a 60 x 20cm rectangle. Leaving a 1cm border, spoon the spinach mixture along the length of the pastry, leaving a 2cm gap at both short ends. Fold in the 2 short ends to stop any of the filling coming out, then roll the pastry away from you to enclose the filling and create a long sausage shape. Join the 2 ends together to create a wreath shape and stick together with a little almond milk. Transfer the wreath to a baking tray lined with baking parchment and chill for 20 mins. Can be made up to this point a day in advance and kept covered in the fridge.

3 Heat oven to 200C/180C fan/gas 6. Using a sharp knife, cut slashes across the top of the wreath. Mix a little almond milk with some olive oil (this will help the pastry colour) and brush all over the wreath. Bake for 40–45 mins until golden brown. Leave to cool for 5 mins, then transfer to a board and decorate with the reserved dill fronds and some dried cranberries.

· ·

Nutrition per serving
Kcals 392 · fat 28g · saturates 8g · carbs 25g · sugars 2g · fibre 3g · protein 8g · salt 0.4g

Vegan pie

Make this fantastic beetroot, sweet potato, chard and celeriac rainbow-layered pie as a stunning centrepiece for a vegan Christmas or dinner party.

⏱ TAKES 2 hrs 45 mins ◔ SERVES 10

FOR THE FILLING
- 80ml olive oil, plus extra for brushing
- 2 tsp ground cumin
- ½ tsp ground cinnamon
- 1 tbsp vegan red wine vinegar
- 3 beetroots (about 400g), peeled and sliced into rounds about ½cm thick
- 1 small celeriac (about 750g), peeled, cut into quarters and then sliced into triangles 1cm thick
- 4 thyme sprigs, leaves picked
- 4 fat unpeeled garlic cloves
- 3 large sweet potatoes (about 600g), peeled and sliced into rounds about ½cm thick
- 2 tsp smoked paprika
- 1 tbsp semolina
- 250g Swiss chard, leaves only (save the stalks to add to soups, stews and risottos)

FOR THE PASTRY
- 150g coconut oil, plus extra for the tin
- 500g spelt flour
- almond milk, for brushing

1 First, make the filling. Heat oven to 220C/200C fan/gas 7. Mix together 1½ tbsp oil with the cumin, cinnamon and vinegar, and rub over the beetroot. Put the beetroot into a roasting tin, season, cover with foil and roast for 20 mins.

2 Meanwhile, toss the celeriac with 2½ tbsp oil, the thyme, garlic and seasoning in another roasting tin. Separate out the slices so they cook evenly, then cover the tin in foil. In a third roasting tin, mix the sweet potato with the remaining oil, paprika and seasoning and cover with foil. Once the beets have cooked for 20 mins, add the celeriac and sweet potato alongside and roast all the veg for 40 mins further or until tender. Remove the thyme, squeeze the garlic out of its skin, mash with the celeriac and leave the veg to cool.

3 For the pastry, boil the kettle and use coconut oil to grease a deep 20cm springform cake tin. Pour the flour into a bowl and add 1 tsp salt. Mix the coconut oil with 200ml boiling water, stir until melted, then pour into the flour and mix with a wooden spoon to form a dough. Working as quickly as you can (it's best to roll it when warm), cut off a ¼ of the dough and set aside under a tea towel. Roll out the rest to 0.5cm thick, then use it to line the tin, pressing the dough into the corners and leaving any excess pastry overhanging the sides. Don't worry if the pastry breaks – you can patch it up as you go. Heat oven to 200C/180C fan/gas 6.

4 Now build the pie. Cover the base with chard, scatter over the semolina (to absorb beet juices), press in the beetroot and season. Add a layer of chard, then sweet potato and season. Add the rest of the chard, celeriac and season.

5 Roll out the pastry you set aside to a thickness of 0.5cm for a lid. Put the lid on the pie and, using a fork, press together the overhanging pastry to create a crimped edge. Make a steam hole and brush the top with almond milk mixed with a tbsp of oil (to help colour the pastry). Bake in the centre of the oven for 45 mins until a deep golden brown. Leave to cool for 15 mins, then remove from the tin and serve. Will keep for up to 3 days in the fridge (the pie is delicious cold).

Nutrition per serving
Kcals 499 • fat 25g • saturates 14g • carbs 53g • sugars 13g • fibre 12g • protein 10g • salt 0.5g

CHAPTER 5: BITES & BAKING

Following a plant-based diet doesn't mean you have to miss out on sweet treats or snacks. We've got cakes and biscuits, savoury bakes as well as healthy snacks to keep you going through the day and stop you reaching for the biscuit tin.

Teriyaki tempeh with peanut dip

Make these tasty teriyaki tempeh canapés ahead of a party and rewarm them in the oven when your guests arrive. Serve with our moreish peanut dipping sauce.

TAKES 25 mins MAKES 16

FOR THE TEMPEH
- 200g pack tempeh
- 1 tbsp olive oil
- 150ml teriyaki sauce
- 40g white sesame seeds, toasted

FOR THE PEANUT DIPPING SAUCE
- 30g peanut butter
- 100ml coconut milk
- 1 tsp chilli flakes
- 1 tsp soy sauce, or tamari
- 1 lime, ½ juiced, ½ cut into wedges to serve
- pinch of sugar

1 First, make the dipping sauce. Mix all the ingredients except for the lime wedges, adding a splash of water to loosen if it is too thick. Season and set aside. Can be made up to a day in advance and kept in the fridge.

2 Cut the tempeh into 16 slices. Heat the oil in a large frying pan over a medium heat. Fry the slices of tempeh for around 3 mins each side. Add the teriyaki sauce to the pan, and turn the slices to coat them. Let it bubble away for 1–2 mins – you're looking for the tempeh to be well covered and sticky.

3 Tip the sesame seeds into a cup. Take the sticky slices of tempeh and push a wooden skewer into each (don't push them down too far). Dip one end of the tempeh into the sesame seeds, then transfer to a serving platter with the dipping sauce in a bowl and the lime wedges on the side.

Nutrition per serving
Kcals 87 • fat 5g • saturates 2g • carbs 6g • sugars 5g • fibre 1g • protein 4g • salt 0.8g

Carrot & caraway crackers

If you're catering for vegans at a party, make these easy carrot canapés that everyone will love. Top with a sprig of dill and a vegetable crisp to impress.

🕐 TAKES 35 mins 🥧 MAKES 20

- 2 tbsp olive oil
- 1 shallot, roughly chopped
- 1 garlic clove, roughly chopped
- 1 tsp caraway seeds
- 400g carrots, roughly chopped
- 300ml vegan vegetable stock
- 20 crunchy vegan crackers (such as an olive oil toast)
- ½ small pack dill, leaves picked, to serve
- 20 veg crisps, to serve

1 Heat the oil in a saucepan over a medium heat. Add the shallot and a pinch of salt and cook for 6 mins until softened. Stir in the garlic and caraway seeds and cook for 1 min more, then add the carrots and veg stock. Bring to the boil and simmer for 12 mins.

2 Once the carrots are completely soft, drain them (reserve the liquid) and blitz to a smooth purée – add a tbsp of the reserved stock initially, but use more if necessary to get the desired consistency. Season and leave to cool. The purée can be made a day ahead and kept in the fridge.

3 To serve, spoon the purée – or, if you want to be extra fancy, transfer it to a piping bag and pipe it – onto the crackers and top each with a little dill and a veg crisp.

Nutrition per cracker
Kcals 60 • fat 3g • saturates 1g • carbs 7g • sugars 2g • fibre 1g • protein 1g • salt 0.1g

Aubergine & chickpea bites

Combine chickpeas and aubergine with garlic and cumin for these tasty, healthy vegan canapés. Everyone will love them served with our harissa yoghurt.

🕐 TAKES 1 hr 20 mins 🥧 MAKES 20

- 3 large aubergines, halved, cut side scored
- spray oil
- 2 fat garlic cloves, peeled
- 2 tsp coriander seeds
- 2 tsp cumin seeds
- 400g can chickpeas, drained
- 2 tbsp gram flour
- 1 lemon, ½ zested and juiced, ½ cut into wedges to serve (optional)
- 3 tbsp polenta

FOR THE DIP
- 1 tbsp harissa
- 150g coconut dairy-free yoghurt

1 Heat oven to 200C/180C fan/gas 6. Spray the aubergine halves generously with oil, then put them cut side up in a large roasting tin with the garlic, coriander and cumin seeds. Season, then roast for 40 mins until the aubergine is completely tender. Set aside to cool a little.

2 Scoop the aubergine flesh into a bowl and discard the skins. Use a spatula to scrape the spices and garlic into the bowl. Add the chickpeas, gram flour, lemon zest and juice, roughly mash together and check the seasoning. Don't worry if the mix is a bit soft – it will firm up in the fridge.

3 Shape the mixture into 20 balls and put them on a baking tray lined with baking parchment, then leave to chill in the fridge for at least 30 mins. Swirl the harissa through the yoghurt and set aside. Can make ahead to this point the day before and keep covered in the fridge.

4 Heat oven to 180C/160C fan/gas 4. Tip the polenta onto a plate, roll the balls in it to coat, then return them to the tray and spray each one with a little oil. Roast for 20 mins until crisp, hot and golden. Serve with the harissa yoghurt and lemon wedges, if you like.

Nutrition per bite
Kcals 66 • fat 3g • saturates 1g • carbs 6g • sugars 2g • fibre 3g • protein 2g • salt 0.2g

Date & walnut cinnamon bites

· ·

These date and walnut cinnamon bites are quick to whip up for a healthy snack. They also work as an after-dinner treat if you have friends round.

🕐 TAKES 5 mins ◔ SERVES 1

- 3 walnut halves
- 3 pitted medjool dates
- ground cinnamon, to taste

1 Carefully cut each walnut half into 3 slices, then do the same with the dates. Place a slice of walnut on top of each date, dust with cinnamon and serve.

· ·

Nutrition per serving
Kcals 168 • fat 8g • saturates 1g • carbs 21g • sugars 20g • fibre 3g • protein 2g • salt 0.1g

Vegan tiffin

Make our vegan tiffin squares as a delicious treat, packed with flavourful ingredients like ginger nuts, dried cranberries and pistachios. They're great for a Christmas party.

🕐 TAKES 20 mins 🕐 MAKES 25

- 75g coconut oil, plus extra for the tin
- 200g vegan dark chocolate (at least 70% cocoa solids), roughly chopped
- 2 tbsp golden syrup
- 200g vegan ginger nuts
- 100g dried cranberries
- 50g pistachios, toasted and chopped

1 Lightly oil a 20cm square brownie tin with coconut oil and line the base with baking parchment. Melt the chocolate with the coconut oil and golden syrup in the microwave in 30-second bursts until smooth and glossy.

2 Break the ginger nuts into small pieces in a bowl, then add the dried cranberries and pistachios. Scrape in the chocolate mixture and give everything a good mix to combine, then spoon the tiffin into the tin. Use the back of the spoon to smooth out the top and press it down, then chill in the fridge for 2 hrs or until set hard. Once set, cut into 25 mini squares. Will keep for a week in the fridge.

Nutrition per serving
Kcals 127 • fat 9g • saturates 5g • carbs 10g • sugars 6g • fibre 1g • protein 1g • salt 0.1g

All-in-one best-ever vegan cookies

Non-vegans would be hard pressed to notice the difference between this and their favourite chocolate chip cookie.

TAKES 30 mins plus 1 hr chilling   MAKES 20 cookies

- 125g cold coconut oil
- 100g golden caster sugar
- 150g light muscavado sugar
- 125ml coconut milk
- 1 tsp vanilla extract
- 275g plain flour
- 1 tsp baking powder
- ¼ tsp bicarbonate of soda
- 200g vegan chocolate chips or vegan chocolate, chopped into small chunks

1 Tip the coconut oil and sugars into a bowl and whisk until completely combined then whisk in the coconut milk and vanilla. Tip the flour, baking powder, bicarb and a good pinch of flaky sea salt into the mix to make a thick batter then fold through the chocolate chips. Chill the batter for at least 1 hr (can be made up to 2 days ahead).

2 To bake heat the oven to 180C/160C fan/gas 4. Line a couple of baking sheets with baking parchment and scoop or roll plum-sized balls of the dough and place them on the baking sheets about 2cm apart. Flatten ever so slightly, sprinkle with a bit more flaky salt if you want, then bake on the middle shelf for 12–15 mins, turning the tray once, until the cookies have spread and are golden but still soft in the middle. Leave to cool slightly then lift on to a wire rack while you bake another batch. These will keep in a biscuit jar for up to 3 days.

Nutrition per cookie
Kcals 221 • fat 10g • saturates 8g • carbs 29g • sugars 19g • fibre 1g • protein 2g • salt 0.12g

Brownies

Soft, squidgy brownies, without the dairy or eggs. Perfect for vegans as well as anyone following a dairy-free diet.

 TAKES 55 mins · MAKES 12

- 80g vegan margarine, plus extra for greasing
- 2 tbsp ground flaxseed
- 200g vegan dark chocolate, roughly chopped
- ½ tsp coffee granules
- 125g self-raising flour
- 70g ground almonds
- 50g cocoa powder
- ¼ tsp baking powder
- 250g golden caster sugar
- 1½ tsp vanilla extract

1 Heat oven to 170C/150C fan/gas 3½. Grease and line a 20cm square tin with baking parchment. Combine the flaxseed with 6 tbsp water and set aside for at least 5 mins.

2 In a saucepan, melt 120g chocolate, the coffee and margarine with 60ml water over a low heat. Allow to cool slightly.

3 Put the flour, almonds, cocoa, baking powder and ¼ tsp salt in a bowl and stir to remove any lumps. Using a hand whisk, mix the sugar into the melted chocolate mixture, and beat well until smooth and glossy, ensuring all the sugar is well dissolved. Stir in the flaxseed mixture, vanilla extract and remaining chocolate, then the flour mixture. Spoon into the prepared tin.

4 Bake for 35–45 mins until a skewer inserted in the middle comes out clean with moist crumbs. Allow to cool in the tin completely, then cut into squares. Store in an airtight container and eat within 3 days.

Nutrition per brownie
Kcals 314 · fat 16g · saturates 6g · carbs 36g · sugars 25g · fibre 3g · protein 5g · salt 0.3g

Millionaire bars

These gluten-free chocolatey treats with dates, cashews and maple syrup are just as sticky and moreish as the original Millionaire's shortbreads.

TAKES 35 mins plus 3 hrs chilling   MAKES 16

FOR THE BASE
- 150g cashew nuts
- 50g rolled oat
- 4 medjool dates, pitted
- 50g coconut oil, melted

FOR THE FILLING
- 350g pitted medjool dates
- 125ml unsweetened almond milk
- 25ml maple syrup
- 150g coconut oil
- 1 tsp vanilla extract

FOR THE TOPPING
- 150g coconut oil
- 5 tbsp cocoa powder
- 2 tsp maple syrup

1 Grease a 20cm square cake tin and line with baking parchment. Tip the cashew nuts and oats into a food processer and blitz to crumbs. Add the dates and coconut oil, and blend again. Transfer to the tin and use a spoon to press the nutty mixture into a compact, even layer that covers the base. Chill while you prepare the filling.

2 For the filling, add the dates, almond milk, maple syrup and coconut oil to a saucepan with a generous pinch of salt and bring to a simmer. Boil for 2–3 mins until the dates are really soft, then tip into the blender, add the vanilla extract and blitz to a smooth purée. Add a little more salt if the mixture is too sweet. Pour over the nutty base and spread to the sides of the tin, getting the surface as smooth as possible. Chill while you prepare the topping.

3 Gently heat the coconut oil in a saucepan until melted. Remove from the heat and whisk in the cocoa and maple syrup until there are no lumps. Cool for 10 mins, pour over the caramel layer and return to the fridge for at least 3 hrs or until firmly set. To serve, cut into squares. Will keep in the fridge for up to 1 week.

Nutrition per bar
Kcals 373 • fat 28g • saturates 20g • carbs 25g • sugars 20g • fibre 3g • protein 4g • salt 0g

Gingerbread people

Switch the butter for coconut oil, eggs for chia and use chickpea water in royal icing to make these easy, totally vegan gingerbread biscuits.

🕐 TAKES 45 mins ◔ MAKES 20

- 1 tbsp chia seeds
- 400g plain flour, plus extra for dusting
- 200g cold coconut oil
- 2 tbsp ground ginger
- 1 tsp ground cinnamon
- 200g dark muscovado sugar
- 50g maple syrup
- 100ml aquafaba (water from a can of chickpeas)
- 500g icing sugar
- ½ tsp lemon juice

1 Put the chia seeds in a small bowl and stir in 3 tbsp water. Leave to soak for 5–10 mins until gloopy. Meanwhile put the flour into a large mixing bowl and rub in the coconut oil until it's almost disappeared into the flour. Stir in the spices.

2 In another bowl mix together the sugar, maple syrup, chia mixture and 2 tbsp water until smooth then pour over the flour. Stir until well combined then knead together to make a soft dough. Wrap in cling film until ready to use.

3 Heat oven to 180C/160C fan/gas 4. Roll out the dough on a lightly floured surface then cut into gingerbread people (or whatever shape you like) and bake for 10–12 mins on baking sheets lined with baking parchment until just starting to darken at the edges. Let them cool for a couple of minutes on the tray then transfer to a wire rack to cool.

4 While the gingerbread cools whip the aquafaba in a bowl using electric beaters until really foamy. Add three-quarter of the icing sugar and whisk until smooth and thick, then whisk in the rest of the icing sugar and the lemon juice. Whisk again until the mixture forms stiff peaks. Transfer to a piping bag until ready to use. Snip a little off the end of the piping bag and use to create designs and faces on your gingerbread people.

Nutrition per biscuit
Kcals 315 • fat 10g • saturates 9g • carbs 52g • sugars 36g • fibre 1g • protein 2g • salt 0.01g

Salted caramel biscuit bars

A healthier take on one of our favourite chocolate bars, these biscuits are packed with wholesome ingredients, and free from refined sugar and dairy.

TAKES 1 hr plus 30 mins chilling MAKES 18

FOR THE BISCUIT BASE
- 80g porridge oats
- 20g ground almonds
- 50ml maple syrup
- 3 tbsp coconut oil, melted

FOR THE CARAMEL FILLING
- 125g medjool dates, pitted
- 1½ tbsp smooth peanut butter or almond butter
- 2 tbsp coconut oil, melted
- ½ tbsp almond milk
- generous pinch of salt

FOR THE TOPPING
- 150g vegan dark chocolate

1 Heat oven to 180C/160C fan/gas 4 and line a large baking tray with baking parchment. For the base, blitz the oats in a food processor until flour-like. Add the remaining ingredients and whizz until the mixture starts to clump together. Scrape into a bowl, then roll and cut into 18 equal-sized rectangular bars, about 9 x 2cm. Place on the prepared tray and use a small palette knife to neaten the tops and sides of each biscuit. Bake for about 10 mins until lightly golden at the edges, then leave to cool.

2 Meanwhile, put all the caramel ingredients in the food processor (no need to rinse it first) and blitz until it forms smooth, shiny clumps. Using a spatula, push the mixture together, then roll into 18 even-sized balls using your hands.

3 Once the biscuits are cool, squash the caramel onto them. Use your fingers to press it into shape and smooth out any bumps, especially around the edges (as they will show underneath the chocolate coating).

4 Melt the chocolate in a heatproof bowl set over a pan of simmering water – make sure the water doesn't touch the bowl (otherwise, it might seize and go grainy). Carefully dip one of the caramel-coated biscuits in the chocolate, turning it gently with a small palette knife (use this to lift it out as well). Use a spoon to drizzle over more chocolate to coat it fully. Let the excess chocolate drip into the bowl, then carefully put the biscuit back on the lined tray.

5 Repeat with the remaining biscuits, then chill in the fridge for at least 30 mins or until the chocolate has set. Put the biscuits in an airtight container and store in the fridge. Will keep for up to 5 days.

Nutrition per biscuit
Kcals 137 • fat 8g • saturates 5g • carbs 13g • sugars 8g • fibre 2g • protein 2g • salt 0.1g

Cupcakes with banana & peanut butter

Employ some clever tricks to achieve a dairy-free bake – egg-free mayonnaise, almond milk and margarine fit the bill.

🕐 TAKES 45 mins ⏲ MAKES 16

- 240g self-raising flour
- 140g golden caster sugar
- 1 tsp bicarbonate of soda
- 240g egg-free mayonnaise
- 2 large or 3 small ripe bananas, mashed
- 1 tsp vanilla extract
- 25g vegan dark chocolate chips

FOR THE ICING
- 80g vegan margarine
- 250g icing sugar
- 25ml vegan milk (we used almond milk)
- 2 tbsp smooth peanut butter

1 Heat oven to 170C/150C fan/gas 3½. Line muffin tins with 16 cases. In a bowl, combine the flour, sugar, ½ tsp salt and the bicarbonate of soda. In a second bowl or a jug, mix the mayonnaise, mashed bananas and vanilla extract. Pour the wet ingredients into the dry and mix with a spoon until just combined (don't overmix or your cupcakes will be heavy). Spoon the mixture into the cases and bake for 20 mins.

2 When the cupcakes come out of the oven, sprinkle the chocolate chips over – they will melt and then harden again, so don't touch them.

3 For the icing, combine the vegan margarine and icing sugar in an electric mixer, then add the vegan milk and continue to mix on a slow speed until completely combined. Turn the mixer up and combine for a further 3 mins. Finally, stir in the peanut butter. Pipe or simply spread the icing on top of the cakes. Store in an airtight container and eat within 2 days.

Nutrition per cupcake
Kcals 295 • fat 14g • saturates 3g • carbs 40g • sugars 28g • fibre 1g • protein 2g • salt 0.7g

Banana bread

Use up your ripe bananas in this banana bread – the perfect breakfast treat to enjoy with your morning cuppa. We love it toasted with peanut butter.

 TAKES 50 mins SERVES 8-10

- 3 large black bananas
- 75ml vegetable oil or sunflower oil, plus extra for greasing
- 100g soft brown sugar
- 225g plain flour (or use self-raising flour and reduce the baking powder to 2 heaped tsp)
- 3 heaped tsp baking powder
- 3 tsp ground cinnamon or mixed spice
- 50g dried fruit or nuts (optional)

1. Heat oven to 200C/180C fan/gas 6. Mash the peeled bananas with a fork, then mix well with the oil and sugar. Add the flour, baking powder and cinnamon or mixed spice and combine well. Add the dried fruit or nuts, if using.
2. Bake in a greased, lined 900g/2lb loaf tin for 20 mins. Check and cover with foil if the cake is browning. Bake for another 20 minutes or until a skewer comes out clean.
3. Allow to cool a little before slicing. It's delicious freshly baked, but develops a lovely gooey quality the day after.

Nutrition per serving
Kcals 218 • fat 8g • saturates 1g • carbs 33g • sugars 15g • fibre 2g • protein 3g • salt 0.5g

Chocolate cake

Make our easy vegan chocolate sponge for a special occasion using dairy substitutes. It's finished with luscious 'buttercream' and seasonal fruits.

⏱ TAKES 55 mins ⏳ SERVES 10–12

- 150g dairy-free spread, plus extra for the tins
- 300ml dairy-free milk, we used oat milk
- 1 tbsp cider vinegar
- 300g self-raising flour
- 200g golden caster sugar
- 4 tbsp cocoa powder
- 1 tsp bicarbonate of soda
- ½ tsp vanilla extract

FOR THE BUTTERCREAM
- 100g vegan dark chocolate
- 200g dairy-free spread
- 400g icing sugar
- 5 tbsp cocoa powder
- 1 tbsp dairy-free milk, such as oat milk

TO DECORATE
- handful of fresh, seasonal fruits such as cherries, blackberries or figs

1 Heat oven to 190C/170C fan/gas 5. Grease the base and sides of 2 x 20cm sandwich tins with dairy-free spread, then line the bases with baking parchment.

2 Put the dairy-free milk in a jug and add the vinegar – it will split but don't worry. Put all of the other cake ingredients into a large bowl, pour over the milk mixture and beat well until smooth. Divide the mixture between the prepared tins and bake for 25–30 mins or until a skewer inserted into the middle of the cakes comes out cleanly. Leave to cool in the tins for 10 mins then turn out onto two wire racks to cool completely.

3 To make the buttercream, put the chocolate into a heatproof bowl and melt in the microwave, stirring every 30 seconds. Leave the melted chocolate to cool for 5 minutes. Beat the dairy-free spread and icing sugar together with a wooden spoon then sift in the cocoa powder with a pinch of salt. Pour in the melted chocolate and dairy-free milk and keep mixing until smooth.

4 Sandwich the 2 cooled sponges together with half of the buttercream then pile the rest on top and down the sides. Decorate with the fresh fruit.

Nutrition per serving
Kcals 606 · fat 30g · saturates 8g · carbs 75g · sugars 53g · fibre 4g · protein 6g · salt 1.2g

Mug cake

Bake a simple vegan mug cake in the microwave – you can have it ready in under 10 minutes to satisfy a craving. Serve with a scoop of dairy-free ice cream.

🕐 TAKES 7 mins 📊 SERVES 1

- 3 tbsp dairy-free milk, we used oat milk
- pinch lemon zest
- 1 tsp lemon juice
- 1 tbsp sunflower oil
- 4 tbsp self-raising flour
- 2 tbsp caster sugar
- pinch bicarbonate of soda
- 4 fresh or frozen raspberries
- coconut cream or dairy-free ice cream, to serve

1 Put the milk in a microwave-safe mug, add the lemon zest and juice and leave to sit for 2–3 mins. It should start to look a bit grainy, as if it has split. Stir in the sunflower oil, flour, sugar and bicarbonate of soda. Mix really well with a fork until smooth.

2 Drop in the raspberries then microwave on high for 1 min 30 secs, or until puffed up and cooked through.

3 Serve with a drizzle of coconut cream, or a scoop of dairy-free ice cream if you like.

Nutrition per serving
Kcals 576 • fat 13g • saturates 2g • carbs 104g • sugars 43g • fibre 4g • protein 8g • salt 1.4g

Lemon cake

· ·

Try baking a vegan version of lemon cake. Light and zingy, it also works well if you replace the flour and baking powder with gluten-free alternatives.

🕐 TAKES 45 mins 🕐 SERVES 12

- 100ml vegetable oil, plus extra for the tin
- 275g self-raising flour
- 200g golden caster sugar
- 1 tsp baking powder
- 1 lemon, zested, ½ juiced

FOR THE ICING
- 150g icing sugar
- ½ lemon, juiced

1 Heat oven to 200C/180C fan/gas 6. Oil a 450g/1lb loaf tin and line it with baking parchment. Mix the flour, sugar, baking powder and lemon zest in a bowl. Add the oil, lemon juice and 170ml cold water, then mix until smooth.
2 Pour the mixture into the tin. Bake for 30 mins or until a skewer comes out clean. Cool in the tin for 10 mins, then remove and transfer the cake to a wire rack to cool fully.
3 For the icing, sift the icing sugar into a bowl. Mix in just enough lemon juice to make an icing thick enough to pour over the loaf (if you make the icing too thin, it will just run off the cake).

· ·

Nutrition per serving
Kcals 276 • fat 9g • saturates 1g • carbs 47g • sugars 29g • fibre 1g • protein 2g • salt 0.3g

Carrot cake

Give free-from baking a go with this easy vegan sandwich cake – an indulgent carrot cake with coconut and cashew icing that everyone will want another slice of.

🕐 TAKES 1 hr 5 mins 🕐 SERVES 12–15

FOR THE ICING
- 4 sachets (200g) creamed coconut
- 1 tbsp lemon juice
- 2 tbsp cashew nut butter
- 50g icing sugar
- 60ml oat milk

FOR THE CAKE
- 250ml jar coconut oil, melted
- 300g light brown sugar
- 1½ tsp vanilla essence
- 210ml dairy-free milk, we used oat milk
- 420g plain flour
- 1½ tsp baking powder
- 1½ tsp bicarbonate of soda
- 1 tsp cinnamon, plus extra cinnamon to decorate
- 1 tsp ginger
- 1 tsp ground nutmeg
- 1 orange, zest only
- 4 medium carrots, grated (you want 270g grated weight)
- 75g chopped walnuts, plus extra to decorate
- edible flowers (optional)

1 Start by making the icing first. Mash the coconut cream with 2 tbsp hot water and the lemon juice until smooth. Add the cashew butter then whisk in the icing sugar followed by the oat milk. Continue to whisk until fully combined, set aside in the fridge until needed.

2 Heat the oven to 180C/160C fan/gas mark 4. Grease 2 x 20cm cake tins with a little of the melted coconut oil and line the bases with baking parchment. Whisk together the oil and sugar, then add the vanilla and milk. Combine the flour, baking powder, bicarbonate of soda, spices and orange zest in a separate bowl. Add these to the wet mixture and stir well. Finally stir in the carrot and the nuts. Divide the mixture between the prepared tins and bake for 25–30 mins until a skewer inserted into the middle of the cake comes out cleanly. Cool in the tin for 5 mins before transferring to a wire rack to cool completely.

3 Sandwich the cakes together with half the icing then cover the top with the remaining icing (add a splash of oat milk if the icing feels too firm). Scatter over the chopped walnuts and dust the cake with a little cinnamon and decorate with edible flowers.

Nutrition per serving (15)
Kcals 501 • fat 31g • saturates 23g • carbs 49g • sugars 26g • fibre 2g • protein 5g • salt 0.45g

Sponge cake

Treat friends and family to a Victoria sponge cake made with vegan ingredients. This easy recipe is perfect for afternoon tea, or a coffee morning.

TAKES 55 mins   SERVES 8-10

- 150g dairy-free spread, plus extra for the tins
- 300ml dairy-free milk (we used oat milk)
- 1 tbsp cider vinegar
- 1 vanilla pod, seeds scraped
- 300g self-raising flour
- 200g golden caster sugar
- 1 tsp bicarbonate of soda

FOR THE FILLING
- 100g dairy-free spread
- 200g icing sugar, plus extra for dusting
- 4 tbsp jam, we used strawberry

1 Heat oven to 180C/160C fan/gas 4. Line the bases of 2 x 20cm sandwich tins with baking parchment and grease with a little of the dairy-free spread.

2 Put the dairy-free milk into a jug and add the vinegar; leave for a few minutes until it looks a little lumpy. Put half of the vanilla seeds and all the other cake ingredients into a large bowl then pour over the milk mixture. Using electric beaters or a wooden spoon, beat everything together until smooth.

3 Divide the mix between the tins then bake in the centre of the oven for 30–35 mins or until a skewer inserted into the middle of the cakes comes out cleanly. Leave them in their tins until cool enough to handle then carefully turn out onto wire racks to cool completely.

4 While the cakes are cooling, make the filling. To make the vegan buttercream, whisk or beat together the dairy-free spread, icing sugar and remaining vanilla seeds until pale and fluffy. Dairy-free spreads do vary so if the spread you are using is quite soft try to avoid using electric beaters and stir the ingredients together instead to avoid overworking it. However, if the mixture is too firm, use electric beaters to help lighten it and then add 1–2 tbsp dairy-free milk when whisking.

5 Spread the jam onto one of the cooled sponges, top with the buttercream then place the other sponge on top. Dust the assembled cake with a little icing sugar or caster sugar before slicing.

Nutrition: per serving
Kcal 482 • fat 21g • saturates 4g • carbs 69g • sugars 45g • fibre 1g • protein 3g • salt 1.2g

Mince pies

Bake these vegan mince pies for a Christmas party, with a cherry and hazelnut filling that everyone will love.

🕐 TAKES 1 hr 40 mins plus chilling 🕐 MAKES 16–18

- 1 large apple (around 200g), peeled and grated
- 200g mixed dried fruit
- 390g jar black cherries in kirsch
- 100g skinless hazelnuts, roasted and roughly chopped
- 1 orange, zested and juiced
- 1 tsp ground cinnamon
- 1 tsp ground ginger
- 1 tsp ground allspice
- 150g soft dark brown sugar

FOR THE PASTRY
- 400g plain flour
- 200g coconut oil, straight from the fridge (as solid as possible)
- 20g icing sugar, plus extra for dusting
- 50ml ice-cold vodka
- 50ml non-dairy milk, for brushing

1 Heat oven to 180C/160C fan/gas 4. Tip all the mincemeat ingredients into a casserole dish or roasting tray – be sure to include half the kirsch from the jar of cherries. Mix everything together, then cover with a lid or a sheet of foil. Bake for 35–40 mins until all the sugar has melted, the mixture is bubbling slightly at the edges and the liquid has reduced (the mixture firms a bit as it cools, so be careful not to over-reduce). Set aside to cool completely. Can be made up to 3 days in advance and chilled in the fridge.

2 To make the pastry: tip the flour and coconut oil into a food processor and pulse until the mixture resembles breadcrumbs. Add the sugar and pulse to just combine, then pour in the vodka and 2 tbsp ice-cold water and pulse until the pastry is just coming together. Add another 2 tbsp water if a little dry, then tip the dough onto a clean surface and pat into a disc with your hands. Wrap in cling film and chill in the fridge for at least 30 mins.

3 Take the pastry out of the fridge. Cut off one-third of the pastry and keep covered under a tea towel. Cut the rest into 5 chunks and, one chunk at a time, squeeze with your hands until malleable, then roll out on a well floured surface to a thickness of 0.5cm. Cut out circles using a 9cm cookie cutter and line 18 holes of two 12-hole cupcake tins. Repeat with the rest of the pastry chunks, re-rolling off-cuts where necessary.

4 Put a heaped spoonful of mincemeat in the middle of each circle, then put the pies in the fridge. Take the remaining pastry from under the tea towel and roll out to 0.5cm thickness. Transfer to a baking sheet lined with baking parchment. Chill for 15 mins to firm up.

5 Heat oven to 180C/160C fan/gas 4. Remove the pastry sheet from the fridge and use an 8cm cookie cutter to cut out 9 circles, then use a star cutter to cut out the middles. Bring the mince pies out of the fridge and top half of them with the stars and the other half with the stamped-out circles. Use your fingers to seal the tops and bases, then brush the tops with milk. Bake for 30 mins until the pastry is crisp and the tops are golden. Cool a little, then dust with a little icing sugar to serve.

Nutrition per serving
Kcals 315 • fat 15g • saturates 10g • carbs 38g • sugars 18g • fibre 2g • protein 4g • salt 0.3g

'Cheesy' scones

Try these dairy-free vegan scones that use nutritional yeast for a cheesy flavour, pepped up by mustard and smoked paprika. Serve with vegan onion chutney.

🕐 TAKES 35 mins 🥧 MAKES 7

- 3 tbsp olive oil, plus extra for the tray
- 1 tsp white wine vinegar
- 250ml almond milk
- 1 cauliflower stalk (around 100g)
- 300g self-raising flour, plus extra for dusting
- ½ tsp baking powder
- 3 tbsp nutritional yeast
- ¼ tsp mustard powder
- ¼ tsp smoked paprika
- 3 thyme sprigs, leaves picked
- vegan onion chutney, to serve

1 Heat oven to 220C/200C fan/gas 7 and lightly oil a baking tray. Mix the vinegar with the almond milk and set aside. Bring a saucepan of water to the boil, add the cauliflower stalk and cook for 5 mins until almost tender. Drain well, leave to cool, then finely chop.
2 Mix the flour, baking powder, nutritional yeast, spices, thyme leaves and 1 tsp salt in a large bowl. Add the cauliflower, then add the oil and pour in 230ml of the soured almond milk. Working quickly, bring the mixture together with a wooden spoon; if there is any dry mixture in the bowl, add more almond milk to make a soft but not sticky dough. Tip the dough onto a floured work surface and pat to a thickness of about 2.5cm.
3 Cut out rounds with a 6cm fluted cutter and transfer to the baking tray. Gather together any offcuts and cut out more rounds.
4 Bake on the top shelf of the oven for 10–12 mins until golden. Serve warm with onion chutney.

Nutrition per serving
Kcals 235 • fat 6g • saturates 1g • carbs 35g • sugars 1g • fibre 3g • protein 8g • salt 1g

Watermelon salsa

Serve this zingy, refreshing watermelon salsa as a dip or pile on top of nachos. Deliciously moreish, it makes a lovely, light summer snack.

🕐 TAKES 10 mins 🕐 SERVES 4–6

- 200g watermelon
- 2 small shallots
- small bunch coriander
- juice ½ lime
- 2 tbsp olive oil

1 Finely chop the watermelon, shallots and coriander. Mix together with the lime juice and olive oil. Season and serve as a dip or pile on top of nachos.

Nutrition per serving (6)
Kcals 46 • fat 4g • saturates 1g • carbs 3g • sugars 3g • fibre 0g • protein 0g • salt 0g

CHAPTER 6: DESSERTS

You'd be amazed at the variety of desserts you can still enjoy if you're following a vegan diet. Using clever substitutes, you'd never know these are made without dairy, eggs or other animal products. Lots of these recipes use a magic ingredient called aquafaba, which is actually just the water from a can of chickpeas. It's packed with protein and whips up just like egg whites, meaning you can use it to recreate some of your favourite desserts.

Chai coconut & mango creams

Vegan, dairy, gluten and nut-free – and delicious – this fruity, delicately spiced dessert will go down a storm at any dinner party.

TAKES 50 mins plus chilling and 2hrs setting SERVES 4

- 4 allspice berries
- 4 cardamom pods
- 1 cinnamon stick
- 3 cloves
- 1 vanilla pod, split, or ½ tsp vanilla extract
- 2 x 400ml cans full-fat coconut milk
- 200g caster sugar
- a little vegetable or sunflower oil, for greasing
- 1 ripe mango, 1 cheek cut into small dice and set aside to serve, remaining 140g roughly chopped
- juice of ½ lime
- 4 tbsp agar-agar flakes
- 2 crinkly passion fruits, to serve
- mint leaves, to serve
- toasted coconut shavings, to serve

1 Put the allspice berries and cardamom pods in a large saucepan. Use the end of a rolling pin to gently split open the cardamom pods and crack the allspice into a few pieces. Add the remaining spices, coconut milk and 140g of the caster sugar to the pan. Set over a gentle heat and simmer for 5 mins. Cool, then chill overnight.

2 Grease 4 x 200ml pudding moulds, ramekins or pretty glasses with a little oil (you can skip this if you don't want to turn the creams out once set). Put the remaining sugar, chopped mango and lime juice in a food processor and blend to a purée. Sieve the purée into a saucepan, sprinkle 1 tbsp agar-agar flakes over the surface and leave to stand for 5 mins or until the agar-agar has dissolved. Stir the agar-agar into the purée and bring to a gentle heat, then simmer for 3–5 mins, stirring now and then, until the purée has thickened slightly. Divide among the moulds and chill for at least 2 hrs or until set.

3 Strain the infused coconut milk into a clean pan and discard the spices. Sprinkle over the remaining agar-agar flakes and leave for 5 mins until the agar-agar has dissolved. Heat gently for 3–5 mins, stirring now and then. Divide the mixture among the moulds and chill for at least 4 hrs, or overnight.

4 To serve, dip the base of each mould into hot water for 10 secs or so, then turn out onto a plate. Top each dessert with a little chopped mango, some passion fruit seeds and a small sprig of mint, then sprinkle the coconut flakes around the plate.

Nutrition per serving
Kcals 626 • fat 37g • saturates 30g • carbs 68g • sugars 64g • fibre 4g • protein 3g • salt 0g

Lemon cheesecake

An easy no-cook cheesecake that's dairy-free and gluten-free with just a little agave syrup to sweeten. A lusciously lemony vegan dessert the family will love.

🕒 TAKES 20 mins plus soaking and chilling 🍰 SERVES 12

FOR THE BASE
- 30g cold coconut oil, plus extra for greasing
- 100g blanched almonds
- 100g soft pitted dates

FOR THE TOPPING
- 300g cashew nuts
- 2½ tbsp agave syrup
- 50g coconut oil
- 150ml almond milk
- 2 lemons, zested and juiced

1 Put the cashews in a large bowl, pour over boiling water and leave to soak for 1 hr. Meanwhile, blitz the ingredients for the base with a pinch of salt in a food processor. Grease a 23cm tart tin with coconut oil, then press the mix into the base and pop in the fridge to set (about 30 mins).

2 Drain the cashews and tip into the cleaned out food processor. Add all the remaining topping ingredients, reserving a quarter of the lemon zest in damp kitchen paper to serve, then blitz until smooth. Spoon onto the base and put in the fridge to set completely (about 2 hrs). Just before serving, scatter over the reserved lemon zest.

Nutrition per serving
Kcals 297 • fat 22g • saturates 8g • carbs 16g • sugars 10g • fibre 1g • protein 7g • salt 0.1g

Sticky toffee pear pudding

A lighter version of sticky toffee pudding, rich with dates and spices, and the juicy texture of poached pears, this vegan dessert is sure to please a crowd.

🕐 TAKES 1 hr 15 mins 🕐 SERVES 8

- 8 small firm pears (we used Conference)
- 200g golden caster sugar
- 2 cinnamon sticks
- 1 star anise
- 6 cloves
- 1 lemon, zest pared
- 1 orange, zest pared
- vegan ice cream, to serve (optional)

FOR THE SPONGE
- 250g pitted dates
- 2 tbsp linseeds
- 300ml unsweetened almond milk
- 200ml vegetable oil, plus extra for greasing
- 175g dark muscovado sugar
- 200g self-raising flour
- 1 tsp bicarbonate of soda
- 1 tsp ground mixed spice

1 Peel the pears and cut the bottom off each to give a flat base – cut them to a height that will fit snugly in your tin. Use a melon baller or small knife to cut out the pips from the base. Roughly chop the pear scraps, discarding the pips, and set aside. Tip the sugar, cinnamon, star anise, cloves, zests and 600ml water into a saucepan large enough to fit all the pears. Bring to the boil, then simmer until the sugar has dissolved. Add the pears, cover with a lid or a piece of baking parchment, and poach gently for 15 mins until a knife easily slides into a pear. Leave to cool in the liquid.

2 Now make the sponge. Put the dates and linseeds in a saucepan and add the almond milk. Bring to a gentle simmer, then cook for 2–3 mins until the dates are soft. Pour into a food processer and blitz until smooth. Add the oil and blend again, then scrape into a bowl and set aside to cool a little. Heat oven to 180C/160C fan/gas 4. Grease and line a 20 x 30cm baking tin (a loose-bottomed one if possible) with a strip of baking parchment.

3 Put the dry ingredients in a large mixing bowl with ½ tsp salt. Mix well, breaking up any lumps of sugar with your fingers, and shaking the bowl a few times to encourage any remaining lumps to come to the surface. Add the date and oil mixture and stir well. Fold in the chopped pear scraps. Scrape the cake mixture into the tin, then nestle in the pears, standing straight up, so that the bottom halves are covered. Bake for 35–40 mins until the cake is cooked through. Insert a skewer to the centre to check – it should come out clean. If there is any wet cake mixture on the skewer, return the cake to the oven and bake for 10 mins more, then check again.

4 Meanwhile, bring the pear poaching liquid back to the boil and simmer until reduced to a glossy syrup. When the pudding is cooked, cool for 5–10 mins, then brush all over with the syrup, saving a little extra to serve alongside, with vegan ice cream, if you like.

Nutrition per serving
Kcals 646 • fat 27g • saturates 2g • carbs 94g • sugars 75g • fibre 6g • protein 4g • salt 0.9g

Ginger & marmalade roulade

Use aquafaba (the liquid from a can of chickpeas) to create a delicious vegan ginger and marmalade roulade. It takes a little effort, but it's well worth it.

🕐 TAKES 40 mins ⏀ SERVES 6

- 360ml aquafaba (the liquid from 2 x 400g cans chickpeas)
- 230g caster sugar, plus extra for dusting
- 1 vanilla pod, seeds removed
- 150g self-raising flour
- 2 tsp ground ginger
- 200g coconut yoghurt or use coconut cream, set aside in the fridge for a few hours before lightly whisking
- 2 tbsp icing sugar, plus extra for dusting
- 150g marmalade
- 2 balls of stem ginger, finely chopped

1 Heat the oven to 190C/170C fan/gas 5 and line a 23 x 33cm Swiss roll tin with baking parchment. Whisk the aquafaba for 6 mins or until it reaches soft peaks, then add the caster sugar and vanilla, 1 spoonful at a time, whisking in between each addition so that the mixture turns to stiff peaks. Sift in the self-raising flour with the ground ginger, then use a metal spoon to fold the flour into the aquafaba mix. Pour into the lined tin and smooth with a spatula so it's evenly spread. Bake for 20 mins until just firm to the touch.

2 While the sponge is baking, lay a piece of baking paper onto a work surface and dust with caster sugar. Once the sponge has baked, turn it out on the sugared paper and peel off the baking paper on the bottom. Allow to cool a little, then use the sugared paper to gently roll up the sponge from the shortest edge. Leave to cool a little longer in the rolled-up shape (this will make it easier to roll up again later), then gently unroll to cool completely.

3 Whisk the coconut yoghurt or cream with the icing sugar until thickened. Once the cake is cooled, spread it with the marmalade leaving a 2cm border, then scatter with the stem ginger. Spread the coconut yoghurt on top, keeping the border, then use the sheet of baking paper again to help you to roll up the sponge back into the rolled shape. Remove the baking paper, trim the ends, then place on a serving dish, dust with icing sugar and serve.

Nutrition per serving
Kcals 421 • fat 7g • saturates 6g • carbs 86g • sugars 62g • fibre 1g • protein 3g • salt 0.3g

Vegan meringues

Whip up some crunchy meringues for a showstopping summer dessert. This recipe uses vegan 'aquafaba' (chickpea water) in place of traditional eggs.

🕐 TAKES 1 hr 35 mins ◷ MAKES 10-12

- 400g can chickpeas
- 100g golden caster sugar

1 Heat oven to 110C/90C fan/gas ¼ and line a baking tray with parchment. Drain a 400g can of chickpeas over a bowl (save the chickpeas for another recipe).

2 Using an electric whisk, whisk the chickpea water to soft peaks, like egg whites. Add 100g golden caster sugar, a little at a time, whisking constantly until thick and glossy.

3 Spoon or pipe the meringue in blobs, about 8cm wide, over the tray. Bake for 1 hr 15 mins until crisp. Leave to cool, then you can pile with soya cream and fruit for a delicious vegan dessert.

Nutrition per serving (12)
Kcals 39 • fat 0g • saturates 0g • carbs 10g • sugars 8g • fibre 0g • protein 0g • salt 0.1g

Chocolate & date tart

Impress your guests with this decadent chocolate and date tart in a shortcrust pastry case. It's sure to go down a treat with everyone.

TAKES 1 hr 10 mins plus chilling and setting SERVES 8

- flour, for rolling
- 320g shortcrust pastry sheet suitable for vegans
- 180g medjool dates, pitted and chopped
- 400ml coconut milk
- 1 tsp vanilla extract
- 200g vegan dark chocolate, finely chopped
- 3 tbsp coconut oil

1 On a lightly floured surface, roll the pastry sheet into a slightly larger rectangle, big enough to line a 20cm tart tin. Line the tin, leaving any overhanging pastry – you'll trim this away once the tart is baked. Chill for 30 mins on a baking tray. Heat oven to 200C/180C fan/gas 6.

2 Line the pastry with greaseproof paper and fill with baking beans. Bake for 15–20 mins, then remove the paper and beans and bake for 15 mins more, until cooked through. Remove from the oven and leave the case to cool in its tin, then trim the sides.

3 While the pastry is cooling, make the date caramel. Soak the dates in 100ml of boiling water for 5 mins. Meanwhile, tip the can of coconut milk into a bowl and give it a good whisk to combine. Drain the dates and put them into a food processor with 150ml of the coconut milk, the vanilla extract and a big pinch of flaky salt and blitz – the mixture should look like caramel. Spread the caramel onto the base of the tart and put in the fridge for 30 mins to set a little.

4 To make the ganache topping, heat the remaining coconut milk over a low heat until steaming. Put the chocolate and coconut oil in a large bowl and pour the warm coconut milk over the top. Leave to sit for a minute, then gently stir until combined. Spoon the mixture over the caramel and spread it out – don't worry if the caramel comes up the sides a bit. Sprinkle with flaky sea salt, then put into the fridge for at least 4 hours to set.

Nutrition per serving
Kcals 395 • fat 27g • saturates 16g • carbs 30g • sugars 17g • fibre 5g • protein 4g • salt 0.6g

Eton mess

Nothing says summer like a sweet, berry-filled Eton mess and this vegan version swaps the egg whites in the meringues for an ingenious alternative.

⏱ TAKES 1 hr 50 mins plus infusing ◔ SERVES 4

- drained liquid from a 400g can chickpeas (aquafaba)
- 100g golden caster sugar
- 500g mixed berries
- 2 tbsp icing sugar
- ½ tbsp rose water
- 400ml vegan coconut yoghurt

1 Heat oven to 110C/90C fan/gas ¼ and line a baking tray with parchment. Whisk the drained chickpea liquid with an electric whisk until white, fluffy and just holding its shape – be persistent, this will take longer than you imagine. Gradually whisk in the caster sugar until your chickpea meringue reaches stiff peaks. Spoon the vegan meringue onto the baking parchment and bake for 1 hr 30 mins, or until it comes off the paper easily. Leave to cool.

2 Meanwhile, mix the berries with the icing sugar and rose water. Set aside for 30 mins so the flavours infuse and the berries release some of their juices.

3 Put the yoghurt into a large bowl, crush in the meringues then stir through one-third of the fruit, rippling it through the yoghurt. Spoon into 4 serving dishes then top with the remaining fruit.

Nutrition per serving
Kcals 383 • fat 19g • saturates 17g • carbs 46g • sugars 42g • fibre 5g • protein 4g • salt 0.2g

Rhubarb & custard bake

Use clever replacements in this dairy-free fruit pudding with soya custard. Serve cold as a cake or warm for pudding.

🕐 TAKES 1 hr 35 mins plus cooling 🕒 SERVES 15

- 250g rhubarb, cut into 2–3cm lengths
- 275g golden caster sugar
- 1 tsp vanilla bean paste
- 250g vegan margarine, plus extra for greasing
- 2 tbsp ground flaxseed
- 150g soya custard, plus extra to serve (optional)
- 250g self-raising flour
- 1 tsp baking powder
- 1 tsp vanilla extract
- 130g unsweetened apple sauce
- icing sugar, to serve (optional)

1 Heat oven to 200C/180C fan/gas 6 and put the rhubarb in a roasting tin. Sprinkle over 25g of the caster sugar, add the vanilla bean paste, give the tin a shake and put it in the oven for 15 mins. Remove, pour away any liquid from the tin and leave the rhubarb to cool.

2 Reduce oven to 170C/150C fan/gas 3½. Grease and line a 25 x 20cm cake tin with baking parchment. In a small bowl, mix the flaxseed with 6 tbsp water and set aside for 5 mins.

3 In a bowl, beat together the margarine, 100g of the custard, the flour, baking powder, vanilla extract and remaining sugar. Once this is well combined, light and fluffy, add the apple sauce and flaxseed mixture.

4 Put a third of the mixture in the tin and top with a third of the rhubarb. Repeat twice more, then dot teaspoons of the remaining custard on top.

5 Bake in the oven for 45 mins, then cover with foil and bake for a further 30 mins or until golden brown and a skewer comes out clean when inserted in the middle. Serve warm as a pudding with soya custard, if you like. Or allow to cool completely, then sprinkle with icing sugar and enjoy as a cake. Eat the same day.

Nutrition per square
Kcals 274 • fat 15g • saturates 3g • carbs 34g • sugars 21g • fibre 2g • protein 2g • salt 0.3g

Cheat's pineapple, Thai basil & ginger sorbet

An easy blended sorbet with vibrant Thai basil and spicy ginger. Try serving with a drizzle of vodka or white rum.

🕙 TAKES 5 mins plus chilling overnight ⏻ SERVES 6

- 1 large pineapple, peeled, cored and cut into chunks
- juice and zest of 1 lime
- 1 small piece of ginger, sliced
- handful Thai basil leaves, plus a few extra little ones to serve
- 75g white caster sugar
- vodka or white rum (optional)

1 A couple of days before eating, tip everything except the vodka or rum into a blender or smoothie maker with 200ml water and blitz until very smooth. Pour into a freezable container and freeze overnight until solid.

2 A few hours before serving, remove from the freezer and allow to defrost slightly so it slides out of the container in a block. Chop the block into ice cube-sized chunks and blitz in the blender or smoothie maker again until you have a thick, slushy purée. Tip back into the container and refreeze for 1 hr or until it can be scooped out.

3 To serve, scoop the sorbet into chilled bowls or glasses and top with extra basil. If you want you can drizzle with something a little more potent, such as vodka or white rum.

Nutrition per serving
Kcals 145 • fat 0g • saturates 0g • carbs • 33g • sugars 33g • fibre 3g • protein 1g • salt 0g

Christmas pudding

Make this vegan Christmas pudding as part of a festive feast, packed with dried figs, raisins, sultanas and a tot of rum. Serve warm with vegan ice cream.

🕐 TAKES 3 hrs 30 mins 🕑 SERVES 12-14

- 125g dairy-free margarine, plus extra for greasing the bowl and paper
- 375g dried figs
- 75ml rum
- 350g mixed sultanas and raisins
- 1 large eating apple, peeled, cored and grated
- 85g light brown soft sugar
- 85g dark brown soft sugar
- 100g breadcrumbs
- 100g self-raising flour
- ½ tbsp allspice

1 Grease a 2-litre pudding bowl with dairy-free margarine, then line the base with a circle of baking parchment. Grease a large sheet of baking parchment, then lay it on top of a large sheet of foil, margarine side up. Fold a pleat in the middle of each sheet.

2 Roughly chop 125g of the figs and set aside. Put the remaining figs, the dairy-free margarine and the rum into a large food processor and whizz until smooth-ish, then scrape into a large mixing bowl. Tip in the chopped figs, sultanas, raisins, grated apple, sugars, breadcrumbs, flour and allspice. Stir everything together, then spoon into your pudding basin.

3 Cover with the buttered paper-foil sheet, tie with string and trim. Lower into a large saucepan, with upturned saucers or scrunched-up bits of foil in the bottom (so the pud doesn't touch the bottom), then fill the pan with enough boiling water from the kettle to come halfway up the sides of the bowl. Cover with a lid and simmer for 3 hrs, topping up the water as needed. Remove and leave to cool. Will keep in a cool, dry cupboard for up to a year.

Nutrition per serving (14)
Kcals 289 • fat 6g • saturates 1g • carbs 50g • sugars 42g • fibre 4g • protein 3g • salt 0.3g

Index

BETTWS

21. 1. 19.